Crime in America

Milton Meltzer

Crime in America

MORROW JUNIOR BOOKS

NEW YORK

Printed in the United States of America.
1 2 3 4 5 6 7 8 9 10

Library of Congress Cataloging-in-Publication Data
Meltzer, Milton, 1915–
Crime in America / Milton Meltzer.
p.   cm.
Summary: Discusses various aspects of crime in America, including
crime in the streets, battered family members, the Mob, and law
enforcement.
ISBN 0-688-08513-X
1. Crime—Juvenile literature.   [1. Crime.]   I. Title.
HV6789.M45   1990
364.973—dc20   90-5698   CIP   AC

Contents

Crime in America

Stop Blaming the Victims in C...

To the Editor:

While I commend
...ape on college camp
...ews (Jan. 1), I am
...me ways your artic
...unrealistic, victim
...ective of sexual assau
Although   acquainta
...ntioned, you never d
...t the problem is, there
...lege men raping, not
...men being raped at co
...st of these assaults tak
...nal social situations i
...d to late in the article.
...e emphasis on security,
...ur report but also on ca
...notes an image of an
...ger breaking into a st
...or assaulting her as she
...dorm, rather than the
...on reality of, for example,
...d plying his date with d
...aking advantage of her''
...oo drunk to resist or consen
...focus on victims rather t
...ators is most egregious wh
...ion is discussed. The poi...
...en that 50 p...

Drug Wars Scar Capital's Chi d...

By B. DRUMMOND AYRES Jr.
Special to The New York Times

WASHINGTON, May 14 — Like soldiers who have seen too much combat,
not increasing numbers of children in the
nation's capital are beginning to show
signs of "battle fatigue" because of un-
relieved exposure to the city's drug
wars.

Educators, psychologists and police
officials report more and more instances when young people act irra-
tionally or need counseling after wit-
nessing or experiencing the drug-related violence in Washington. That violence has led to 300 deaths and almost
50,000 arrests in the last two and a half
years.

Psychologists tell of children who
talk of death, who have learned to
avoid eye contact with passers-by, wh
can tell the kind of gun being fir
...the block by its sound. Teache...

A Losing Fight On Violence In the Schools

New York City, S...

The Helmsleys Are Cha
With $4 Million Tax E...

By RONALD SULLIVAN

Harry and Leona Helmsley evaded
more than $4 million in income taxes
by fraudulently charging such luxuries
as a marble dance floor above a swim-
ming pool, a $45,000 silver clock and a
$130,000 stereo system to ...
...and real-estate empire to ...tel
...id yesterday

Mrs. ...

suppliers and contracts
crime that carries a max
of 20 years in prison.

The Helmsleys and tw
financial aides pleaded
their arraignments in S
Court in Manhattan. All
leased without posting bai

Mrs. Helmsley, is
head of the hotels, is wide
...er iron composure, whic
...ined for a while in court
...aited arraignment wi
...d, tears welled in her e
...iging her mascara.

...ments in Pentagon Case
Expected After Election

...N, Oct. 29 (AP) — Fed-
...rs expect to bring the
...ts in the Pentagon fraud
...vestigation shortly after
...al election, according to the
...rosecutor in charge of the

...optimistic on mid-Novem-
...nts,'' said Henry E. Hud-
...ed States Attorney in sub-
...nia who is running the
...multi-agency investiga-
...Department officials fix
...Nov. 15, which is the next
...rand jury is scheduled to

...n said he would have pre-
...uments sooner.

investigators have reviewed 700,000
documents and more are under sub
poena to be turned over Th
tened to "thre...
...tap...
...cer...
...fou...
...cou...
...the c...
...eign...
...''alw...
...consu...

Mr. ...
...cludin...
...tions, a...
...Federa...
...Naval...

Addiction's Hidden Toll:
Poor Families in Turmoil

By PETER KERR

As crack causes crime rates to
soar and drug bazaars to infect
...ment's street corners in New York and
other major cities, the smokable
form of cocaine is taking a hidden
but far more devastating toll, ex-
...tearing apart what

Meanwhile, in the same neighborhoods where the relatively
stable heroin industry thrived for
decades, crack has suddenly
created drug organizations and
gangs that vie for control of a
volatile new market with a level

Art, Antiques and
Federal
...to yet...

...ed Scheme Evades Millions in Gas

By SELWYN RAAB

...Moskowitz was
...tly re...

The tax evaders, call
cheat by creating dum
and false documents
...compan...

k's Hidden Toll: The Destr...

Costing Small Businesses $1 Billion a Year, a Study Sho

...EVESI

...serious toll on
...ew York City out-
...ting them more
...limiting the num-
...create and forcing
...r close, a recent

...all Business, Big
...ace, a public policy
...ion, concluded that
...sive effect on small
...York City with 83.1
...companies surveyed
...ey had been hit by
...ree years.]

...sman, Lieut. Robert
...department officials
...ecause they had
...stanley E...

said the study "gives credence to our
outer-borough strategy of bringing
jobs to where people live."

"Our efforts to relocate and help
businesses expand in the outer bor-
oughs creates activity," Mr. Grayson
said, "and activity deters crime." Despite budget constraints, he said, the $6
million allocated for those activities
would not be cut in next year's budget.

Lost an Average of $22,019

The Interface study was paid for by
the Robert Sterling Foundation, the
New York Foundation and the New
York Community Trust, and was prepared with the Coalition for Neighborhood Development, representing 15,000
small businesses. The study will be
made public today.
...study said the 350 companies
...age of $22,019 —

or a total of $7.7 million — because of
crime over the last three years. Stanley S. Litow, the executive director of
Interface, said when that average is
applied to the 85,000 small businesses
outside Manhattan, those companies
would have lost $500 million a year
over the last three years.

At the same time, the 350 companies
spent an average of $8,385 a year on se-
curity. "If you project that over the
85,000 firms, those businesses spend
another $600 million on security each
year," Mr. Litow said.

Declining Sales

And there is also a social cost. The
number of jobs being created by small
businesses in New York City is about
one-third the national figure. A 1987
Federal Bureau of Labor Statistics
study showed that small businesses

create 66 percent of new jobs in
...tion. But, in New York City,
...count for only 22 percent.

The study said 11.6 percen
companies surveyed reported
canceled plans to expand be
crime.

Asked about other effects o
their businesses, 17.8 perc
companies surveyed said sa
clined; 16.7 percent said
hours were reduced; 19.3 pe
they were considering relo
9.1 percent said they were
closing.

The businesses survey
average of 27 employees.

The most common ty
against small businesse
said, are break-ins, va
and truck theft and b
shoplifting.

1

No Easy Answers

CRIME?

We all worry about it. It's talked about in the press, on the job, at the kitchen table. Politicians promise a new war on crime every time they run for office. They know what people fear the most.

Sadly, it's true that one way or another, crime touches the life of every American. More than twenty years ago a presidential commission on crime warned: "There is much crime in America, more than ever is reported, far more than is ever solved, far too much for the health of the nation."

Driven by their fear, people turn their homes into fortresses, with bars over windows, multiple locks on doors, electric alarms, high fences, watchdogs. In apartment house lobbies and corridors, TV cameras and intercom systems guard against intruders. Car owners paste stickers on the window saying, No Radio or Tape Deck! Public buses display signs warning, Driver Does Not Carry Cash. To protect the cab driver from theft, thick glass or caging wire separates the driver from the passenger in the back-seat. Will private citizens soon have to put on bulletproof vests as they leave for work?

Crime is no new plague. Long before our time it ravaged people worldwide. In every society, in every century since humankind evolved, there have been thieves and murderers, rapists and gangsters, swindlers and extortionists. The history of every people tells us of criminals who preyed upon their fellow beings and broke the law of their land.

How is crime defined? One source says it is "behavior that violates the criminal laws." As laws change from time to time, and from place to place, the behavior that may be called criminal varies greatly. Except, perhaps, for certain basic acts such as murder, robbery, and assault. The criminal, then, is a person who does something society defines as going beyond the limits of legally accepted behavior.

There are many kinds of crime:

- *Crime in the streets.* This is what people fear the most. It includes robbery, mugging, burglary: the purse snatched, the pocket picked, the necklace torn off, the store or home broken into and ransacked. Much of this is now done by people hooked on drugs who desperately need money to pay for another fix.

- *Organized crime.* This is perpetrated by professional gangs who traffic in drugs, extortion, loansharking, prostitution, gambling. They buy off officials, and they don't hesitate to use force to get what they want.

- *Crimes of passion.* This category covers the acts of people whose emotions under stress overcome their ability to reason. Most murders, rapes, and assaults fall into this category.

- *Violation of regulations.* People break the rules meant to protect the public health, safety, and convenience. Driving or walking through a red traffic light, ignoring a building code or a fire ordinance, failing to observe minimum standards of quality when providing goods or services, breaking safety laws, misrepresenting products or services. All of this is antisocial conduct that can cause injury, illness, or death. It is usually a form of the white-collar crime listed next.

- *White-collar crime.* This huge category of offenses is often ignored or goes unpunished. Yet tax evasion, price fixing, embezzlement, consumer fraud, and swindling run through society, especially at its higher and most respectable levels. It costs the nation and the public billions of dollars every year.

- *Corruption in public office.* Almost daily the media report bribes, payoffs, fixes, conflicts of interest on every level of government—local, state, federal—and in every branch of public service, including the police force. Officers commissioned to protect society and its citizens are sometimes guilty of wrongful arrest, brutality, blackmail, racism, and numbers of other crimes.

It's hard for people to think coolly when it comes to crime. We react with intense emotion—especially when we ourselves have been the victim of a crime. Then, too, the violent crimes that are the nightly sensation of the local TV newscasts and the daily diet of the hometown newspapers fill us with horror. Other kinds of crime get much less attention. Yet all crimes are tied together, threads in the fabric of the society we live in. To focus on the murder, the mugging, the rape, the robbery, while ignoring all the others produces an oversimplified picture and unworkable solutions.

Crime has to do with the way we manage our society, run our own lives, and connect with one another. It has to do with human behavior. It is people who commit crimes. Crime has to do with personal conscience and social morality. Crime is not an isolated problem. It is not merely "bad guys" doing in "good guys."

Ramsey Clark, a man who knew crime intimately as attorney general of the United States in the 1960s, put it this way:

Crime reflects more than the character of the pitiful few who commit it. It reflects the character of the entire society. How do people capable of stealing a car or mugging a cripple, of embezzling from the bank that trusted them or raping an eighty-year-old woman, come to be that way? All they are and all they have experienced that drove them to commit that crime overcame all that sought in vain to restrain them. What they are and what they experienced came largely from society—from its influence on them and their forebears.

Crime is a huge subject, so huge that thousands of studies have been published about it. This short book cannot attempt to cover every corner of the story. But it will take up some of the important questions people seek answers to:

- Just what are the known facts about the extent of crime?
- What kinds of criminal actions are there and what kinds of people commit them?
- What are the causes of crime and what is the cost of crime to American society?
- What kind of criminal justice system do we have, and how effective is it?
- What can be done to reduce the amount of crime?

None of these questions have easy answers. The experts—criminologists, sociologists, psychologists, police, lawyers, judges—sometimes hold a common view; more often they disagree. So what this book will try to do is explore their findings and opinions. In this way, readers will get a clearer idea of crime and what might be done about it.

E OF FOUR HOM.
T BY CRIME IN

of North—

Rise in hate crime generates

Crimes motivated by prejudice are on the rise again.
The Anti-Def—
B'na: Fi—

New York

Nears Reco

For Slaying

obberies Drop 26% Since Worst

By SARAH LYALL

obbery, which some experts say is
... safe a city is,
best indicat
... York
s dropped
here since 198
ty since 198
e drop to
omputer tra
and other re
But, while
effective a
neat their
the has al

Under the prog
brought to the sta
ately and shown
dreds of known r
The police have
robbers ofter
in the sa

Police in New
York City credit
ecial units and

Drugs and Heat Ci
74.8% August S

th drug u
e grace
rs wer

Capital's Homicide

By IRVIN MOLOTSKY
Special to The New York Times

WASHINGTON, Oct. 28 — With two
months left in the year, Washingto
has already matched the record o
icides set in 1969, and the
of drugs

Record

More Robberies, More Arrests

Number of reported robberies and arrests in the New York City subway system each month.

Robbery Arrests
1987 1988

Robberies
1987 1988

urder Ramp
rofessionals Re

By Naomi Thiers
Staff Writer

ited States has a higher
rate than any industrial
the world. Eve
rders ar

son as
problems
lationship c
it's just too

600
500
300
200
100
her
Europe

Jan. Feb. Mar. Apr. May Jun. Jul.

Jan., Feb., Mar. Apr. May Ju

Source—New York City

ays Violent Crime
ped From '80 to '84

York Times
y 8 — The United
percent decrease
om 1980 through
s here were still
se in Western Eu
the Government

Declines are
noted in homicide
an

Crime in New York:
Midyear Figures

Percent change in reported crime in the first six months of 1988 from the similar period in 1987.

Murder and manslaughter	+ 7.7%
Rape	− 5.6
Robbery	+ 8.0
Aggravated assau	+12.5
Tota aga	

Murder and Manslaughte
To Near-Record in New

Continued From Page 1

street in stranger-to-stranger encounters."

No figures have been compiled showing where the murder rate would rank New York among American cities, police officials said. Last year, New York ranked ninth in murder and manslaughter among the 25 largest cities, with 1,672 killings. Jacksonville, Fla., was eighth, and Detroit first, with a two and a half times that of New Orleans was second. The tal numbers, but

The largest six-month
rests was for motor
Forty percent more
seized this year than i
months of 1987, from 5,32
Over all, police arres
the first six months of
last year's period, Chie
The total reported crim
percent over the first six
year, and arrests for a
up 7.2 percent.

Grim Picture by

Chief Hoehl said that
be surprised at all if the
increase" in the July an
tics, although he was "h
increase will be down, a
bout reductions
Mayor

RISE
RK CITY

anslaughter Are
ecord Levels

VID E. PITT

ork City Police Depart-
yesterday that murder
ghter rose to a near-
in the first six months of

considered an import
in assessing overall cri
ercent higher in the firs
of the year, compared wi
period a year ago, accord

ust two months, May a
umber — including rob
me — rose shar

Atlanta, Used to Praise, Confronts Crime

By PETER APPLEBOME
Special to The New York Times

ATLANTA, April 26 — After years of
promoting itself as one of the nation's
premier centers for economic growth,
Atlanta now finds itself trying to refute
figures indicating that it leads the nation in something less enviable: crime
Last month, amid a bar
licity about crim
in the

nary crime statistics for 1988 from the
Federal Bureau of Investigation
showed Atlanta with the nation's leading rate of violent crimes.

Distortions in Figures S

Atlanta offic
dista

other cities. For in
distributed by the F
showed 77

☞ 2 ☜

The Plain Facts
on Crime

WHILE THERE IS great public concern with crime, the facts about it are not widely known. The first job, then, is to find out what the real dangers are, not the imagined ones. What we know about crime rates comes from three official sources. The Federal Bureau of Investigation (FBI) publishes annually the Uniform Crime Reports. The U.S. Justice Department's Bureau of Justice Statistics makes surveys of the inmates of prisons, and the same department, together with the U.S. Census Bureau, conducts a criminal victimization survey. These sources provide nationwide data on arrests, imprisonment, and victimization. (You can find the data in the *World Almanac* under "Vital Statistics.") Occasionally, other groups, such as the 1967 President's Commission on Crime, publish a good deal of information on crime.

Here are some of the facts found in recent government reports. The most precise figures are for arrests. These are collected each year by the FBI from local law-enforcement agencies. For example, in 1987 there were 10,795,869 arrests. Listing eight categories of crime as serious, the FBI provides these figures: 16,714 for murder, 31,276 for rape, 123,306 for robbery, 301,734 for aggravated assault, 374,963 for burglary, 1,256,552 for larceny, 146,763 for motor vehicle theft, and 15,169 for arson. Drug abuse violations (not listed under "serious"), 811,078. These are figures for arrests, not convictions.

According to the Justice Department, there were 547,000 inmates in our state and federal prisons in 1988. Another 275,000 men and women were awaiting trial in local jails or serving short terms there. And 2.4 million people were on probation or parole for crimes they had committed. To get some idea of the proportion of people netted in these figures, recall that the total population of the United States in the late 1980s was about 240 million.

The plain numbers are important, but they don't explain much about crime. Social scientists add to our understanding by their systematic research in criminology. They analyze official crime statistics and the methods of recording crime data. They study what kinds of criminal offenses occur, where they take place, and what kinds of classes of people commit which crimes. They compare the social backgrounds of known offenders with groups of non-offenders closely matched for background. They ask the general public about the kinds of things they've done that could be considered illegal. They study the life history of juvenile delinquents as well as adult professional criminals. They examine the way youth gangs are formed and how they operate. They look at the different kinds of prisons and treatment programs and try to measure their effects. You could say that just about every aspect of criminal behavior and the public response to it has been, and is being, explored.

It is not easy to determine crime rates and to see what trends are developing. But the facts at hand today do indicate that crime in the United States is growing. The FBI says that crimes reported for 1987 showed an increase of 2.2 percent from 1986. Most researchers believe the crime level now is higher than normal for a modern Western industrial society. (But what is "normal"? No one knows.)

Newspapers sometimes headline a "crime wave." Again, that phrase lumps all crimes together; it doesn't draw the important line between the various types. Besides, it's inaccurate to speak of "a crime wave," for as Attorney General Ramsey Clark said, "a wave periodically recedes but crime didn't—it just kept increasing."

Many criminologists believe that more crimes are committed than are reported. A true picture (but an impossible one to produce) would include the total number of crimes committed, both the unreported and the reported. An apparent rise in crime is sometimes due to the greater readiness of victims to report certain kinds of crime (such as rape or child abuse), as well as the greater willingness of the police to keep better records.

The police also deal with so-called peacekeeping offenses—drunkenness, disorderly conduct, vagrancy—and these are huge in number, far more numerous than the major crimes. Taking action against such offenses makes up a large part of police activity. These offenses aren't listed in the official crime figures. Nor can the official figures cover unreported criminal behavior. When the President's Crime Commission of 1967 made a survey of victims, it found far more victims than officially reported. Rapes were over three times the number reported, burglaries three times, assaults and larceny more than double, and robbery 50 percent greater than the reported rate. Where illicit behavior is private and by consent of the parties concerned—gambling, illegal drug sales, prostitution—the offense is most likely not reported.

The police are never told about a good deal of shoplifting, minor embezzlement, and petty fraud. About 90 percent of the victims of consumer fraud say they don't bother reporting it to the police. So it's clear that official figures do not reflect the actual extent of criminal behavior. What the reports do represent is a combination of what offenders actually do and what the police learn about such crimes and then choose to record. To debate crime trends or to speculate about whether the modern world sees more crime than earlier societies is probably a useless exercise. What can be said once more, however, is that the experts agree crime in the United States has increased considerably between 1933, the year national data were first gathered, and now.

One survey made by the President's Crime Commission reported that 91 percent of all Americans have violated laws that could subject them to a term in prison. Of course, not anywhere near that number are arrested or brought to trial.

The Crime Commission concluded that "what people have to fear most from crime is in themselves: their own carelessness or bravado, their attitudes toward their families and friends; toward the people they work for or who work for them; their appetites for drugs and liquor and sex; their own eccentricities; their own perversities; their own passions. Crime [consists] of the brutal, frightening, surreptitious, selfish, thoughtless, compulsive, sad, and funny ways people behave toward each other."

Don't Even Think of Stealing This Radio

By SARAH LYALL

Christopher Conquest's first car stereo was a portable boom box that he kept in the back seat. It was stolen in 1980. He bought a new car and had a stereo radio and cassette tape player installed. That unit was stolen last year. He had a third unit installed. It was stolen several months ago.

"The first time, I was demoralized, and after that, I was angry," said Mr. Conquest, a human-resources consultant who ~~in Stamford but often drives his~~ ~~New York City, and says he~~ ~~driving without music. Now~~ ~~o unit, he removes it~~ ~~arks, leaving in~~ ~~" sign.

creasingly brazen and sophisticated, a the police have not made a signific dent in the problem.

The Police Department does not k specific figures on how many car ra and tape players are stolen each But in response to a growing feelin thefts are increasing, they recently tuted an anti-theft program in whi components will be marked with ible ink for identification. Using a violet light, they say, the police able to tell if a radio or tape pla been stolen, and its owner will ge

"All car crime is on the way Detective John Eanniello of th ment's auto crimes division. son, very simply, is crack.

"They're out there and the thing for money," he said of addicts. "The easiest way t break into a car, rip the rad quick $10 or $20 and get a lucrative mark

on Page

The police have a new identification program.

Continued From Page B1

car components. Petty criminals, and more organized theft rings, often take radios and tape players to junkyards, selling them for as little as $15 a unit. They are resold to body shops for $50 or $100, and then to consumers, who might pay $250 to $500 for a radio that originally sold for $800.

Demand for used radios and tape players remains high, in part, because so many car owners have had their own stolen.

"The thieves not only steal the radio, but they create a market for it — the guy that had the radio stolen needs a new one," said Thomas J. Russo, who owns a body shop in Brooklyn.

No One Has Exact Figures

In the first six months of this year, there were 32,899 reported instances of what the police call "larceny of vehicle accessories," thefts of car parts including bumpers, dashboards and radios. At the current rate, the 1988 figure would be slightly higher than that for last year, when 61,775 cases were reported.

Conversations with victims and law-enforcement authorities suggest that the number is higher, partly because those victims without insurance do not report the thefts. "There's really been a dramatic increase — you can tell that by walking around the streets," said Sgt. Robert Tellone of the Police artment's crime prevention divi-

get calls about thefts and car windsmashed in every day," said Rosenblum, the district manager

of Community Board 7 on the Upper West Side of Manhattan. "People are breaking into cars now even if there are no radios and they have the sticker saying, 'No Radio.'"

Experts say that radios and other components are more likely to be stolen from cars in densely populated residential neighborhoods, while cars in more remote areas are more likely to be stripped or stolen altogether. Some of the prime targets for radio theft, Detective Eanniello said, are midtown Manhattan; the Sheepshead Bay and Bensonhurst sections of Brooklyn, and Forest Hills, Queens.

Signs Proliferate

Several weeks ago, the police began the citywide program that seeks to prevent thefts of radios and other audio components by marking them with indelible, invisible ink that can be seen under portable ultraviolet lights. Cars are marked prominently with stickers identifying them as members of the program.

The program is so new that the police have no statistics yet to measure its success. But until now, car owners say, they have been frustrated by the apparent inability of the police to solve a problem that seems only to be worsening. Rather than deal with the police,

they have been appealing to the wo be criminals.

In some areas, nearly every seems to have a "No Radio" sign in window. The signs are becoming mo plaintive and elaborate, often listin things the car does not have ("No Radio, No Air-Conditioning, No Computer") or disparaging the worth of what it does have ("Lousy radio").

'This Has Gotten Ridiculous'

Mass-produced "No Radio" signs are on sale at the State Department of Motor Vehicles' branch office in Brooklyn, at 333 Schermerhorn Street. More and more car owners have bought radios and tape players that can be secured out of sight in the car, in a glove compartment or a specially designed strongbox; radios that do not work unless a particular code is punched in, or radios that can be slipped out and removed from the car.

"Some people park their car, and they take the radio out, then they take the hubcaps off and remove the steering wheel," Detective Eanniello said. "There's got to be a point where you stop and say, 'This has gotten ridiculous.'"

In a city where nearly everyone with a car seems to have his own tale of burglary or break-in, there is a story making the rounds that may or may not be true. It is the story of a car owner who parked and left a "No Radio" sign in the windshield.

When he came back, he found that all his windows had been smashed, his "No Radio" sign had been turned over and, on the other side, someone had written, "Get One."

3

Crime in the Streets

THE EXPERTS often use robbery as the best indicator of how safe a city is. Robbery is the taking of money or property from a person by force or threat of force. (Seven of eight crimes involve property.) Robbers often use knives or guns, and sometimes their victims are hurt or killed.

New York is the city that consistently reports more robberies than any other city. The FBI says it is second only to Detroit in the number of robberies per 100,000 people. (Crime figures are often given in this ratio—the number of crimes per 100,000 people. That makes it possible to compare the picture in places that have different populations, as in this New York/Detroit example. Absolute numbers without the ratio would be very misleading.)

In the late 1980s, robbery dropped a little in New York City. The police credited the drop to new antirobbery teams, computer tracking of robbery patterns, and other recent innovations. These methods proved effective against robbers whose crimes run in patterns. But the drug-related robbery that has become most common is almost impossible to predict or prevent. Nor does it display a pattern. Therefore, the overall robbery rate remains high everywhere.

In New York City's crime report for 1987, robberies were ranked fourth among seven major felonies. They occurred less often than purse snatchings and other grand larcenies, car theft or burglary, and more often than assault, rape, or murder. While robberies declined slightly in 1987, killings rose. Murders increased by 5.8 percent to 1,691. Crack contributed significantly to that increase; it figured in more than 38 percent of the homicides.

In the cities, thefts of car radios and tape players have become commonplace. Car owners take elaborate measures trying to thwart thieves who manage to find ingenious ways to get around them. Pushed by the rise in such thefts, the New York City police in 1988 began an antitheft program. Car components are marked with invisible ink for identification. Using an ultraviolet light, the police say they will be able to tell if a radio or tape player has been stolen and to restore it to its owner.

Crack is the reason for the rise in car crime. Most addicts will do anything for money, and the easiest way to get it is to break into a car, rip the radio or tape deck out, and sell it for a quick dollar to pay for crack. The price spirals ever higher as the stolen equipment moves on. The criminal takes it to a junk dealer who pays as little as $15 for a radio. Then it is resold to a body shop for several times as much and finally to the consumer, who pays $150 to $500 for a radio that originally sold for $800. So the thief not only steals the radio but creates a market for it. The person whose radio is stolen goes out and buys a replacement.

In just six months, the New York City police received nearly thirty-three thousand reports of theft of car accessories—including bumpers and dashboards as well as radios. The real number is even higher, for uninsured victims often don't report thefts. Cars in less densely populated neighborhoods are more likely to be stripped or stolen altogether. The police report that some people park their cars, take out their radios, take the hubcaps off, and remove their steering wheels. Going the rounds is the story of a car owner who parked his car and left a No Radio sign on the window. When he returned, he found all his car windows smashed, his No Radio sign flipped over; on the back of it were the words, Get One!

In cities with large underground transit systems there is constant war against subway crime. Turnstile vandals and token thieves all but took over some New York City subway stations in 1988. There was an increase, too, in the robbery of passengers. In recent years, crime and fear of crime led to such a decline in the public's belief in subway safety that hundreds of thousands of passengers gave up on the subway in favor of buses and private cars. Once again, crack plays a great role. Much of the increase in subway robbery occurred in neighborhoods where crack-related crime had soared.

The real rise in crime was bad enough, but the fear was made worse by the public's exaggerated notion of crime. Surveys showed that subway passengers on a typical day thought there were four times as many crimes as actually committed. Many using the vast underground system found it easy to imagine being helpless victims of crimes of violence.

Such crimes do occur, of course, and they stir our most primitive fears and prejudices. Fear drives people to move their homes, switch their routes to work, alter their hours on the street, cut down their night activities, change their jobs. Corporations consider fear of crime by employees when they decide where to locate their offices or expand their operations.

Yet people face other kinds of danger far more frequently than crime, and without worrying about it. Heart disease will victimize twice as many women as rape. The odds are thirty-two times greater that a car accident will do injury than that a serious assault will. According to official data, only a tenth of all crimes are violent.

But violence in its worst form—murder—is, nevertheless, devastating not only to the victims and their families, but to the peace of mind of the community. The United States has a higher homicide rate than any other industrial country. In the 1980s about 20,000 murders a year were committed in the United States. Each year 10 Americans of every 100,000 were murdered. In West European countries the homicide rate was fewer than 2 per 100,000. Taking Australia, Canada, and New Zealand together, the homicide rate was less than 3 per 100,000.

Violent crime shows ups and downs over the years, changes that the experts find it hard or impossible to explain. A study for the years 1980 through 1984 reported a 21 percent decrease in violent crimes in the United States. But the rate was still much higher than for Western Europe in that period. Homicide, rape, and robbery were four to nine times more frequent in the United States than in those countries. Comparisons could be made because in all these places crime definitions and reporting practices were similar.

America's decrease in violent crime between 1981 and 1984 did not continue. In New York City, for instance, murder and manslaughter rose to near-record levels in the first half of 1988. Robbery, assault, and theft all rose sharply, too. Calling the numbers "very, very bad," the city's crime commission said that "the murder statistics told you about the drug warfare in the streets, which we have certainly not gotten under control, by any means."

Bad as the situation in New York was, it was worse in other cities. In 1987 New York ranked ninth in murder and manslaughter among the twenty-five largest cities. Detroit was first (with a rate two and a half times that of New York), and New Orleans was second in rates per 100,000 people.

In New York the rate of all crimes involving attacks on people—murder, manslaughter, forcible rape, robbery, aggravated assault—rose nearly 10 percent in the first half of 1988. Crimes involving property—burglary, larceny, and motor vehicle theft—went up about 8 percent. The police department noted that in the early 1980s, 20 to 25 percent of the homicides were drug-related. But in 1988, nearly 40 percent were, or almost double. "All the studies show that people tend to become more violent when they use crack," said a police official.

Why is murder so prevalent in the United States? The rate is so stunning to foreign observers that they consider murder an American disease, an epidemic. Those who study the problem describe two classes of homicides. They use the term *expressive murder* for those murders committed in the heat of emotion against a relative, friend, or acquaintance. They call it *instrumental murder* when deadly violence is used to get something, such as money, from another person. FBI data consistently show that from two-thirds to three-fourths of American murders are of the first kind. The killings occur most often among people who know each other.

But don't people in other countries find themselves in similar situations, feeling great emotional pain or anger? Then why don't they commit murder as often as distressed Americans? Dr. Carl Bell, executive director of the Community Mental Health Council in Chicago, has studied the phenomenon of murder in the United States. He believes that the easy availability of guns is a major reason for the rate of expressive murder. He found that the handguns many Americans keep in their homes are 118 times more likely to be used on a relative or friend than against an intruder.

Dr. Bell gives Detroit as one example of what happens when people get scared, buy a gun for protection, and then end up shooting a member of the family. After the 1968 riots in Detroit following the assassination of Dr. Martin Luther King, Jr., gun ownership shot up 400 percent in that city. Detroit's murder rate went up from 100 per year before the riots to 700 per year thereafter.

The use of force to solve problems is deeply rooted in American life, many historians believe. It has long colored popular thinking. It's a "shoot-'em-up culture," Bell believes. An argument, a quarrel, a difference of opinion, and "You go for your gun." Violent resolutions to crises seem to be more acceptable in the United States than in other countries.

A ten-year study of criminal violence in 110 countries has been made recently by two university investigators, Dane Archer and Rosemary Gartner. They concluded that violence increases in countries that have just finished fighting a war. The murder rate in the United States doubled between 1962 and 1972, the years we were fighting the war in Vietnam. The rate reached a plateau from which, however, it has not yet dropped.

Other studies indicate that people's economic situation affects murder rates. Poorer people are more likely to be victims of murder or guilty of murder. The more poor people there are, the greater the chance that violence will be used to get money or property. A society with very rich people and vastly more poor people is especially open to violent crime. So much so that Dr. Everett Koop, a former U.S. surgeon general, targeted murder as a major public health problem that the United States must do something about.

mden Journal

n Struggles of the City,
Children Are Casualties

By TAMAR LEWIN
Special to The New York Times

CAMDEN, N.J. —
.Except for a cou-
ple blocks of down-
town, Camden
looks like a war
zone, with block after block of burned
buildings, collapsing buildings, half-
gutted buildings, boarded-up build-

The young
dreams aliv
poverty ar
violence.

Doctors' Group Acts to A

WASHINGTON, Jan. 3 (AP) — The
leading association of obstetricians
and gynecologists today opened a campaign to help women who are victims
of physical abuse, a problem that C
Everett Koop, Surgeon General
United States, said
"overwhelmin

tors report cases of abused w
said that could hurt women h
ing retaliation by
time when

Park Case Puts Focus on Tough Juve

eys were better equipped to prosecute
niles and insisted on more strin-
But since the law was
cases have been
ually with

mit violenc
courts
penalt

**Juvenile-Offender Law:
How It Has Worked**

Total Arrests

1,800
1,600
1,400
1,200
000

When do crimes of
violence deserve

Why Our Society Is Rape-Pr

When Co
Take Cha
Of the Un

the movie "Saturday Night Fever."
There, one boy lures a girl into the
back seat of a car so that a whole
group can have sex with her.
The April 19 incident also shares
some characteristics of "gang
bangs" in fraternity houses and random violence against women on col-
campuses.
understand this form of male
, we must understand the dif-

ference between
and those that
study of 150
Peggy Sanda
found high inc
sociated wit
sonal violenc
of male tou
child relat

Rape-fi
hand, en

By TAMAR LEWI

Last spring, Brenda Va
year-old Washington wom
guilty to forging about $7
checks. It was her first offe
that would normally ha
probation. But because M
was pregnant and tests sho
used cocaine, the judge sen
until the date the baby was
he wanted to protect her
drug abuse.

Ms. Vaughan, who was t
perior Court in the District
bia, was released after
shortly before the birth of
The case has rekindled deb
the increasing use of both c
and drug laws to prosecute w
take illegal drugs while preg
to take their newborn bab
from them.

Hood
E. N.M.
eight

Sad Legacy
Of Abuse:
The Search
or Remedies

es aim to learn why
d childr

ison as
e commit-
by males
w commenta-
r and what
Amer

Suppose
Feared

By Ned Beatty

LOS ANGE
ate is kind. Most
don't have to live
the fear of being
experience t
n't do

Obligation of Protection

"We're seeing a lot more
volving these issues," said D
Chavkin, a physician who has
ller Foundation grant to s
rights an

rug Abuse in Pregnancy: A Conflict Over

Continued From Page A1

ded and illegal, unconstitution-
lying the laws more harshly to
t women than to others. They
what is needed to combat the
sing number of drug-addicted
s is a greater commitment to
ment programs for pregnant

ashington judge who se
. Vaughan

with violating the drug laws. When Ms.
Hudson gave birth on Nov. 13, hospital
urine tests showed that both she and
the baby had cocaine in their bodies.
In Nassau County, Long Island, the
County Department of Social Services
investigates the family of any newborn
whose urine tests positive for drugs, an
indication that the mother had taken
drugs within 72 hours of delivery. Th
department can then

Pregnant drug
users may face
prosecution and
loss of the b

treatment when y
been exposed to c
n't intervene in a
cially when we ha
fer, and we put ba
ments that pose

y New York Can Do More on Child Ab

quick answer that's readily available. The
problems are complicated and need a
combination of approaches, but it is possi-

Mayor
his ad-

vestigated 58,000 complaints of abuse and
neglect last year and monitored 20,000
families at any given time. Nevertheless,

statements and said the city
more than other states." Bu
what new steps he should do

Battered Women, Battered Children

THERE IS VIOLENCE in the street—and violence in the home. Only in recent years has this other kind of violence come to public attention. Nearly one out of every three American families experiences domestic violence. At least 1.8 million women are battered by their husbands every year.

The Victim Services Agency in New York, supported by both private and government grants, has gathered statistics on domestic violence. They reveal that half of all couples have at least one violent incident. The national rate is one every 18 seconds. And it is not a two-way street. More than 95 percent of all spousal assaults are committed by men. Battering as the cause of injuries to women exceeds rapes, muggings, and even auto accidents.

An extraordinary number of men feel free to be emotionally and physically abusive to women. Sociologists attribute this in part to the shortage of men since World War II. With only 81 men for every 100 women, a good many women have trouble finding a man who will commit himself to them. The men feel they have the upper hand; they can pick and choose and call it quits without worry over finding another partner. The women who depend on them have fewer options, so they put up with abuse.

If the abuse becomes too great, however, women may strike back violently. Wives kill their husbands just about as often as husbands kill their wives. But when women kill, studies show, the chances are seven to one that they act in self-defense. The *battered wife syndrome* is a defense now widely accepted by the courts.

Crimes of violence committed by adult females are growing at a faster rate than violence by males. Some female robbers make a professional career out of crime. Far more get involved in a crime when they are drunk or deceived by a lover or in terrible personal trouble.

Women get arrested for aggravated assault, too. That means a crime that results in serious physical injury. About one of every eight such assaults is committed by a woman. Many of these crimes arise out of a personal relationship. Not many women deliberately and coldly beat or torture their victims. Their act is more likely to be the result of a sudden explosion in an intensely personal relationship, when the woman feels she has been cruelly hurt and then hits back.

More than 1.6 million children are abused by parents. Some experts believe this kind of crime is even more widespread than these numbers indicate. That is because abuse of children by parents is often considered a family matter, something no one else should interfere with. People don't want to get involved in trouble next door. Yet everyone is affected: friends, neighbors, employers, taxpayers, citizens. Such violence has consequences that extend into the next generation. For children who suffer violence at home often turn violent against the community. Nearly three-fourths of the people convicted of violent crimes grew up in violent homes.

Many millions of women are now single mothers with at least one child under five years of age. Such mothers, often poor and uneducated, have frequently been exploited or abused by men. They are often ignorant of child development. They expect little kids to know the difference between right and wrong, to do what they're told when they're told to do it. When their children don't obey, frustration boils up into rage in these young mothers, and they abuse their children. Children raised this way may in turn grow up to treat their kids the same way.

Child abuse appears to be growing rapidly, but that may simply be the result of increased media attention and greater readiness to report it. The *battered child syndrome* did not come to public attention before the early 1960s. Not until 1974 were laws adopted requiring the reporting of all suspected child-abuse cases.

What about the crime of rape?

The definition of rape is simple: rape occurs when the act of sex takes place without one partner's consent. Rape is not only a criminal act but a violation of a person's civil rights. Women have the right to choose their sexual partners, to say no if they don't want to be intimate, and to defend themselves when attacked.

The FBI recently estimated that one in ten women will be raped during her lifetime, and one in four girls will be sexually assaulted before the age of sixteen. Any woman can be raped, regardless of her age, race, or occupation. Rapes can occur anywhere; half of all reported rapes occur in the victim's home. Men and boys are raped, too, by other men, but women and girls are the primary targets.

The crime of sexual aggression is related to the beliefs many men hold about violence and male dominance. It is linked to cultural factors—the way men are brought up and the general acceptance of violence.

In one recent study, 40 percent of the men surveyed by a researcher at the University of California in Los Angeles (UCLA) said they might force a woman to commit sexual acts against her will if they could get away with it. Then the question was rephrased, using the crime word *rape.* Still, 15 percent said they might commit such an act if they knew no one would find out about it.

In another study, at the University of Connecticut, researchers examined actual behavior and attitudes toward sex of 175 male college sophomores. They found the majority admitted using coercive tactics to have sexual relations with a woman. They used drugs or alcohol, they used verbal manipulation, they used anger, they threatened force, and 20 percent had actually used force.

These findings agreed with a 1980s Kent State survey of more than seven thousand students at thirty-five colleges. One of every eight women on these college campuses said an acquaintance or date had forced her to have sex at some time, and one of five women said such an attempt had been made. Only 10 percent of these *acquaintance rape* victims told the police. We can conclude, then, that at least ten times more rapes occur among college students than are reflected in official crime statistics.

Jane Hood, a sociology professor at the University of New Mexico, wrote that "several recent surveys of high school students found 40 to 50 percent of both boys and girls agreed with statements such as 'If a girl goes to a guy's apartment after a date, it's OK for him to force her to have sex.' . . . In rape-prone societies rape is confused with sex."

Our culture manages to ignore the high degree of rape by belief in a series of myths about it:

- Rape didn't really happen (the woman was lying).
- Women like the violence of rape (so there's no such thing as rape).
- Yes, it happened, but no harm was done (she wasn't a virgin).
- Women provoke it (men can't control themselves).
- Women deserve it anyway.

Date rape can be brushed aside when such myths prevent people from facing the truth. The impact of these myths is so vicious that 50 percent of the victims of rape don't realize that a crime has been committed against them. An even higher percentage of the perpetrators of rape don't recognize that they are committing a felony when they have sex with an unwilling partner.

Another myth is that most rapes are committed by strangers in dark alleys. It's hard for people to accept the fact that 90 percent of rape victims know their attackers.

Several researchers have found that films portraying extensive violence against women may lead many viewers to accept the rapist's attitudes. Such films as *The Texas Chain Saw Massacre* can make viewers become more callous. These "slasher" movies feature graphic scenes of bloody violence, mainly against young women. At repeated showings of such films men found them less upsetting and more enjoyable and often judged the rape victim to be at fault for what happened. The linking of sex and aggression in the films could lead people to combine sex and aggression in their own lives, according to experimental research by Professors Neil Malamuth of UCLA and Edward Donnerstein of the University of Wisconsin.

In addition to the macho attitudes toward women, there is the factor of individual experience. More than 90 percent of rapists in one study were found to have been the victims of sexual abuse as children. "Getting even" may be a reason for their sexual behavior as adults.

Boy, 11, With 411 Crack Vi...

...rack, Bane of Inner City, ...s Now Gripping Suburbs

By ANDREW H. MALCOLM

which has been devastating
...ner-city neighborhoods, has
...laim significant numbers of
...nd upper-class addicts, ex-
...found.
...ministration drug policy of-
...many law-enforcement ex-
...maintained that crack is
...ly an inner-city problem,
... has indicated that occa-

sional use of drugs, including co
is declining among the more afflu
But now doctors, counselors
crack addicts themselves — in
moving personal accounts — r
substantial increases of addi
among affluent and middle-inc
Americans with a variety of sp
problems.

'Smoking Their Brains Out'

The director of a
ment center
amon

...cher, Kathleen Roach,
she discovered 411 vials
Arricale said. The au-
the crack was worth
n the street.
...ho has a mild learning dis-
... special education
...cipal's of-
...had

the children because of their ag
The boy's 18-year-old half
was not at home yesterday
police sought him for questioni
"We're trying to ascertain
kid came to possess that much
said Lieut. Charles Kammer
the housing police.
The housing police are inve
the case because they were
...ched to the school, which
... project.
...rs on the boy's ble
...ow houses and sr
...ngs described h

Crack Territory: It's What O... Call Their H...

By MICHAEL WINERI...

Monumental Baptist is one of this
ing black churches. On Sunday morni
members fill the pews. There used to l
evening service, too, but the Rev. Willa
ley cut it out. Too many church people
getting mugged by crack dealers.
The minister asked for help, but the po
said they were stretched too thin. "We we
havi... a week stolen," Mr. Ashley si
Nov... few members skip serv
...of the mini
...and t

Speed's Gain in U... Could Rival Cra... Drug Experts W...

By JANE GROSS
Special to The New York Time...

SAN FRANCISCO, Nov. 2...
in a growing number of
laboratories, the drug spee
across the West and could
crack elsewhere in the na
forcement officials and
drug treatment say.
"It's an astronomical pr
Ron D'Ulisse, an agent o
rug Enforcement Adm
Diego and an autho...
... be overstated.
...ment out h
...of contro
...amp

...eading Web
articles.

Users... AIDS DANGER RISES FOR COCAINE USERS

Virus Is Spreading Faster Than... With Heroin — Peril Is in... • Contaminated Needles

By BRUCE LAMBERT

The AIDS virus is spreading
...t faster among people who inject co
...s...ce new research conducted in S
...po... isco and New York City.
The research, not yet
...ific journals, confir
...1 become a
...ion of the
...expert
...ck the
...caine
...ren
...r

...cocaine and c
U.S. based o
038 people in
14 in 1988.

12 million
on
...Addicts
862,000
...Towns

Family Court Judge Fin... 10-Year-Old Did Sell Crac...

By ERIC SCHMITT
Special to The New York Times

HAUPPAUGE, L.I., Feb. 1 — A 10-
year-boy was led away in tears and
handcuffs today after a Suffolk County
judge ruled that the youth had sold
crack from a brown paper bag had
drug-plagued street in Wyandanch last
month.
The judge, Donald L. Auperin of
Family Court, ordered that the boy
continue to be held in a juvenile jail
until the disposition of the case — the
Family Court equivalent of sentencing
— on Feb. 10. In doing so, Judge

...in, in a departure from Family Court
procedure, opened the proceedings.
Judge Auperin's decision followed
two-day fact-finding hearing
which a county police offic
Family Court equivalent of a tr
panion on Jan. 15 tes
rested the boy and a 14-
year-old had dra...
pocket and dr...
The bag co
of crack
boys

...p the Drugs! ...lamor Rises ...oss Jersey

By MICHAEL WIN...RIP

JERSEY
two years Attorney General
...ds — a likely Repub...
...rnor — ha...
...uper...

Pleas for the boy's releas... denied.

New York, Haunted By Crime, Fights for I...

...CIA R. LEE

...ck where Norris Gra-
...ak stretch of sidewalk
...is more for dying than
...and glass are every-
...one has spray-painted
...Dog and Mother" on a

... Graham became the
...rder victim for the 75th
...East New York section,
...has a New York City pre-
...than 100 homicides before
...week.
...ork, site of a Tactical Nar-
...ffort that started Tuesday,
...unofficial homicide

Washing...

By B. DRUMMOND AY...
Special to The New York Tir...

WASHINGTON, Dec. 8 —
two years, the Washington
made more than 44,000 ar
cotics charges in what is
most aggressive and w
drive against drugs in the
As a result, the city tha
quarters of the Governm
wide anti-drug fight he
rate of drug-related
major city in the United
rests per 1,000 residen
...Baltimore, 12 in New

keep out killer

☞ 5 ☜

The Hell of
Addiction

WHAT BOTHERS PEOPLE MOST?

When asked about housing, schools, jobs, people will answer, "Drugs!"

"Do something about it!" is the cry heard all over the country.

Take New Jersey—what one reporter calls "the same old drugged Jersey"—drug arrests keep going up: 40,000 in 1986; 50,000 in 1987; 66,000 in 1988. That sounds like police action, and it is. But has the drug problem diminished? In Jersey City, one of the leading black churches no longer holds Sunday evening services; too many churchgoers are mugged by crack addicts on the way home. A group of thirty-five churches gave the police the addresses of crack houses they wanted closed. Police officers started at the top of the list, did surveillance, made arrests. The hallways emptied out. Then the police moved on and the hallways filled up again with crack dealers.

The staggering load of drug arrests nationwide is pushing the criminal justice system to the limits of its capacity to handle them. It makes it much harder to try other kinds of crime. Few people recall that only a generation or so ago most drugs were used by a small number of criminals and aimless rich kids trying pot. Today the habit has devastated many of the lives of the vastly more numerous poor.

Look at the facts. In 1987, Americans bought an estimated 178 tons of cocaine, 12 tons of heroin, and more than 600,000 tons of marijuana. Between 1983 and 1986 hospitals saw a 167 percent jump in cocaine-related emergencies, while cocaine-related deaths jumped 124 percent in the same period. Why the stunning increase in drug abuse? Price is one reason. A crystal of crack, the cocaine derivative, goes on the street for as little as $5. Get hooked, and addicts lose all moral restraints and their common sense. They sell food stamps, steal TV sets and car radios, and even peddle their child's body for another "escape" with crack.

It's an old story—seeking relief from poverty, from pain, from going up blind alleys, from boredom, from loneliness. Drug addicts get relief swiftly, and briefly, from that desperate dose of a drug. Life isn't beautiful, as they hoped it would be, their dreams haven't come true. So they give in to the false promise of dope—hashish, opium, crack, speed—and find themselves trapped in the hell of addiction.

The problem is immense and grows worse. It does not

affect only the poor. Middle- and upper-class people become addicted, too. But their problem is more easily concealed from public view. Senator Claiborne Pell of Rhode Island estimated that about 20 million Americans have tried cocaine, with 5 million of them regular users, and up to 1 million Americans are cocaine addicts. An additional 500,000 are addicted to heroin.

Senator Pell has said that more than half the criminal cases waiting to be tried in the courts involve drug-related crimes. The National Institute on Drug Studies claims that "one in six American workers is impaired by drugs." It notes that "the hazards of illegal drugs extend far beyond the individual user. Your drug-impaired employee is not just a danger to himself. He's also a threat to fellow workers. Studies show that drug-related industrial accidents involving both users and non-users are increasing." Some experts have estimated that drug and alcohol abuse are adding more than $100 billion to costs of the nation's employers in lost production.

A 1989 congressional report on the drug crisis estimated that 70 percent of all violent crime in the United States is drug-related. The cost in homicides alone is high. By the end of 1988 Washington, D.C., had reached a record high for murders. The police said increased use of drugs, especially crack, was more and more a cause. Quarrels between buyers and sellers, fights over selling in particular areas, and slayings committed while under the influence of drugs were all factors. Some of the victims were innocent bystanders shot dead as rival drug dealers exchanged gunfire.

The drug trade is responsible for tearing apart fragile

ghetto families. A 1988 study of New York City's poorer neighborhoods, where women are often the heads of households, showed that so many women had become crack addicts that child neglect and abuse cases had risen dramatically. In 1988 the number of cases of child neglect or child abuse in New York City was 55,160, up from 46,700 in 1987. City officials also noted a great rise in the number of infants abandoned in city hospitals, born addicted or with syphilis, as well as a rise in children beaten and killed by drug-addicted parents.

With the move from heroin to crack, the illegal drug trade—a multibillion-dollar industry—has enjoyed vastly higher profits. Crack is cheaper and the sales are greater. As new drug gangs compete for control of the market, the level of violence climbs higher and higher. Crack addicts, the police report, are more likely to commit crimes against people than against property.

New York City offers only one example of how the drug craze destroys families and children. The mayor of Alexandria, Virginia, stated, "Every day, drug dealers are fighting turf battles in our neighborhoods with automatic weapons and huge payoffs. The war we are fighting is over the hearts and souls of our young pepole. Drugs are killing our young people." A 12-year-old girl wrote, "Some teenagers can't say no because of what their friends might think of them if they don't use drugs." Young drug pushers or runners recruited by big operators make huge sums of money, wear expensive clothes, and drive flashy cars. They become the envy of classmates, who want to drop out and follow their example. These youngsters are put on the front lines of sales to hide the big dealers. The teenagers, if arrested, are treated like juvenile offenders and given light sentences; they are soon back on the job. Often they carry a gun to protect themselves from rival "stickup boys." The danger is great: shootings over drugs are common, as other people try to rob the runners. "Rarely a day goes by," says District of Columbia delegate Walter Fauntroy, "that does not begin or end with the death of a child, a teenager or a young adult as the result of violence associated with drugs."

In the Miami area, "crack use has spread like wildfire," according to the *Christian Science Monitor*. "What began among the young has become epidemic among their mothers. The hold of crack on women in their twenties and thirties is seriously disrupting the lives of their children."

Wherever crack has taken hold, it has most severely damaged the poorest black and Hispanic neighborhoods. But the addiction also reaches into both black and white working-class areas. It has begun to spread to the middle and upper classes, too, although figures on the numbers of such users are not yet available. (The damage crack does to the affluent is far less visible.) Social workers with drug-treatment agencies observe that the devastation of crack is swift and brutal. Heroin addicts decline more slowly over a five-, six-, and even eight-year period, but with crack, it's "a crash-and-burn kind of thing."

To the link already established between drug abuse and crime, a new link has been added—AIDS. The term is an acronym that stands for *a*cquired *i*mmune *d*eficiency *s*yndrome. It is an infectious, transmissible disease in which the body's immune system is damaged in varying, often progressive, degrees of severity. As a result, persons with AIDS are vulnerable to a number of serious, often fatal, secondary infections or malignancies. The AIDS virus is spreading even faster among people who inject cocaine than among heroin users, according to recent research reports. The reason for the much higher infection rate among cocaine users is that they often inject the drug several times an hour, while the typical heroin addict injects that drug much less often. This means the odds are considerably higher that the cocaine addict will share a needle with a user who has the AIDS virus. Contaminated needles are a leading factor in the spread of AIDS. The virus is also spread by sexual intercourse and is passed through the bloodstream of infected women to their unborn children in pregnancy.

While law-enforcement officials and drug-treatment experts struggle with the problem of crack, another drug threatens to spin out of control. It is speed, or methamphetamine, also known as "crystal," a powerful stimulant to the nervous system. It isn't new: people began using it a generation ago as a diet pill. Then it was diverted to illegal use, and recently it leaped into mass popularity. The off-white powder is coming out of makeshift laboratories in forms that can be snorted, injected, taken in a drink, or smoked. The drug is cheaper than crack and gives a high that lasts longer. It's not hard to make and brings high profits.

Speed's renewed abuse began in the West and Southwest and is moving across the country. Huge amounts are made in hundreds or even thousands of illegal laboratories, and for every lab that is shut down by the authorities, several more open up. Drug rehabilitation centers are jammed with speed addicts. Reports indicate a growing number of speed-related homicides and an increase in drug-induced psychoses. Physicians see a sharp rise in a pattern of agitated, violent behavior in addicts.

Speed presents new problems for law enforcement. Cocaine starts from a plant grown overseas, but speed is made from chemicals right here at home. The makers can do without Bolivians or Colombians to grow the stuff and sneak it into the United States from South America. They simply need the basic chemicals, easily found in the United States. So if attempts to stop or cut down on the flow of cocaine from abroad were ever to succeed, speed could readily take its place. By the end of 1988, both crack and speed were gaining in use at the same time. It's an "astronomical problem," warns the federal Drug Enforcement Administration.

JAMAICA'S GANGS TAKE ROOT IN U.S.

Diminishing on Island, Thugs Are Linked to 1,400 Drug Slayings in America

By JOSEPH B. TREASTER
Special to The New York Times

KINGSTON, Jamaica — A few years ago the police in Jamaica were at war with violent gangs that roamed the desperately poor slums of the capital.

"We carried out some massive assaults on these guys in 1983 and 1984," said Sam McKay, Jamaica's police commissioner for 1985 we were particularly and we began to see the g and die."

Many of the gang member killed or arrested. Some United States, where they gangs that they called "po

Today, the Jamaican p of the most vicious crim America, Federal law en ficials say. They are ma of cocaine and guns, th thorities say, and have b more than 1,400 drug-rel the United States in years.

304 Federal A

The United States At Thornburgh, say Jamaican g members op State Fe

---

Mafia Gang Indicted in East

By SELWYN RAAB

An organized-crime gang that authorities say terrorized an Upper East Side neighborhood through murder, extortion and loan sharking was indicted yesterday under a new antiracketeering law.

For over two years, five key members of the gang engaged in violence, mainly in the vicinity of First Avenue and East 60th Street, the indictment said. Two gang members were accused of luring a rival loan shark to a restaurant in February, shooting him in the head and dumping his body in the East River.

The five men were identified as members and associates of the Gambino crime family, which the F.B.I. has said is the largest, most powerful Mafia group in the country.

A Casino on First Avenue

The indictment also accused gang members of demanding $50,000 from a landlord who objected to their use of his building at 1122 First Avenue as a casino, of assaulting a merchant who refused to turn over his store to the gang's leader as an office and of demanding four apartments from another landlord by threatening her and her children.

The apartments, at 338 East 61st Street, were given to the gang or rented to mem

---

Mob Role in New York Construction De

Special to The New York Times

WASHINGTON, April 29 — Organized crime controls 75 percent of the construction industry in New York City through its control over the concrete industry and construction unions, an admitted mob captain told Senators today.

Vincent (Fish) Cafaro, a former captain in the Genovese organized-crime family in New York, told the Se Permanent Subcommittee gations that the Mafia r ing bids in the city b percent kickback from and their unions

"Legitimate guys chance," he said.

He explained that the sy ranged by the "Two Percent organization run by som York's largest mob families. ses, Gambinos, Luccheses

ers After Valachi

he last of s
ers to t

25 years after Joseph F. Valachi described to the panel the Mafia's vas criminal enterprises.

Mr. Cafaro, a slight, h from the Bronx, has involved with 1958. In 198 the G

Salerno, Now Serving 100 Years, Gets 70 More in Bid-Rigging Case

By The Associated Press

Anthony (Fat Tony) Salerno, the reputed former boss of the Genovese crime family who is already serving a 100-year sentence, was sentenced yesterday to another 70 years in prison in a racketeering conviction.

"That woman needs a psychiatrist," muttered the 77-year-old Mr. Salerno after Federal District Judge Mary Johnson Lowe imposed sentence. "A dred and seventy years."

Salerno was convicted May 4 of ing a massive racketeering hid that included construction tion and gambling. He is year sentence from a 1986 onviction in the trial.

officials now be me family is run e.

Three others were sentenced Thursday. Matthew (Matty the Horse) Ianniello, 68, also a reputed Genovese family member, was sentenced to years in prison and fined $505,000. Edward Halloran, 47, a concrete plier who also once owned The H ran House hotel, was sentenced years and ordered to give up his est in the Certified Concrete Co. Nicholas Auletta, 55, a West businessman, was sentenced years and was ordered to forfe terest in S&A Concrete.

Mr. Salerno was also fined $376,000 and ordered to sur the gross profits from the prise, which the governm into the tens of millions. "There ain't that muc world," he said as he w The four were conv 13-month trial and ar sentenced today. cotivictions. The oth Prosecutors pro bids on many proj than $30 million the Jacob K. Jav 35-count they also on, labo king

---

U.S. Moves In on Fulton Fish Market

By SELWYN RAAB

day later this month, in the ours before dawn, a group of ors will assemble near the Market in lower Manhat out a mission against the

a heavily armed raid ers, the investigators flets among hundreds merchants. ot in the latest Fed e reported organ at the market, the at a court-desig ith broad inves powers, is now the largest country.

H. Wohl, equest of Manhat a new ed to rket

ef. ministrator selected to monitor a major business or industry for Mafia infiltration under the 1970 racketeering law.

A former Federal prosecuto Wohl, in an interview, said h e investigators and office near the weeks

Organized crime, believed to be in control, is the target.

ward T. Furgeson 3d and Allan N. Taf fet, said in court papers last month. Mr. Wohl was appointed under civil provisions of the Federal Racketeer In fluenced and Corrupt Organizations Act, known as RICO. In the last two years some form of court-ordered su pervision has been imposed on four union locals — two in New York City, one in northern New Jersey and one Philadelphia — after Federal prosecu tors proved in court that officials of those unions were linked to organized crime figures.

5 Investigators Hired

Mr. Wohl, however, is the first ad

ple in the market know who we are, what our functions are and how to con tact us."

Since being appointed, Mr. Wohl is 46 years old, said he had been trying to learn "the basics" — how the mar ket functions and the extent of illegal activities.

He said his prime goal was to insure that the market "works smoothly and efficiently," and he promised not to im pose any regulations without first con sulting with the affected merchants.

1,500 People Involved

Some 1,500 people, including whole salers, their employees, truckers, load ers, fish unloaders of supplies, retail throng the market five nights a week, starting around midnight.

For over a century, the pungen stalls and warehouses on the River just south of the Broo have been the center of fish industry in th politan area shellfis

☞ 6 ☜

The Mob Takes Over

WE HEAR MUCH about "crime in the streets" but far less about organized crime—except when some movie about the Mafia catches public attention for a time or a "pizza connection" mob trial lingers on the front pages. Organized crime involves thousands of criminals who operate outside the control of government. The local core group may be known as the "outfit," the "syndicate," or the "mob." What they all want is money and power—just like law-abiding businesses and individuals. Organized crime operates by its own standards and procedures, private and secret ones it creates for itself, changes when it sees fit, and administers ruthlessly.

There is hardly an American whose life is not affected by organized crime. But because it operates secretly, most of us do not realize how we are affected, or that we are affected at all. The price we must pay for any number of the things and services we buy or use is often higher because of a conspiracy by organized crime. But we have no way of knowing that. "If organized criminals paid income tax on every cent of their vast earnings," said the President's 1967 Commission on Law Enforcement, "everybody's tax bill would go down, but no one knows how much."

One reason organized crime flourishes is that it supplies a large number of people with goods and services they want—drugs, prostitution, the chance to gamble, desperately needed cash. From supplying such otherwise unfilled desires at a price come the profits. These are consensual crimes, for the most part. Many people want these things or services, whereas they don't want to be mugged, to have their TV set stolen, or to have their home broken into. It's public demand for these goods and services that creates opportunities for organized crime.

The organized criminals are formed into groups or "families," each with its boss. His underlings carry out the boss's orders and report to him directly. A boss stakes out his own territory and gets a piece of all the criminal activity within it—gambling, prostitution, loan-sharking, drug trade.

Because their enterprises are illegal, organized criminals do everything to keep their activities hidden. Unlike legitimate business with its elaborate system of records and accounting, crime bosses operate far more loosely. Obviously it would be dangerous to keep written records of illegal enterprises. So the collection and the distribution of huge amounts of cash are handled informally, on a personal basis, at some headquarters, social club, or restaurant.

The crime families operate for the most part in the big cities—for example, New York, Chicago, Miami, Los Angeles. Often they have links through kinship or intermarriage. The families all use similar structures and methods. There is not believed to be a ruling council, but on occasion the heads of the more powerful families get together to work out differences that might otherwise lead to bloody internal struggles—always bad for business.

As in any sizable organization, division of labor is found. Criminals showing particular skills will come to specialize as money movers, enforcers, corrupters, executioners. One informer reported that a ten-man squad committed murders for several families, with each killer paid a regular weekly salary.

Just as big a field for organized crime—some experts say even bigger—is extortion of both illegitimate and legitimate business. The mob forces "protection" on enterprises of all kinds. The bar or restaurant is in danger of being stink-bombed or fire-bombed or smashed up if it doesn't pay off. A manufacturer has to buy goods and services from organized crime's supplier or have his property damaged or himself crippled. Money is loaned to a businessman in desperate need of cash he can't get from a bank, at exorbitant interest, and if the debt is not paid on time, he winds up in the hospital. Or he may find he has a new partner, the criminal. In his book *My Life in the Mafia,* Vincent Teresa said his money-making activities included burglary, armed robbery, receiving and selling stolen property, fixing horse races, selling lottery numbers, and running gambling junkets. His specialty was swindling businessmen and banks. But he didn't handle illegal narcotics—only because his boss disapproved.

Today organized crime controls many kinds of production and service industries and businesses. It has also invested part of its illegal profits in legal enterprises. There are some products with respected brand names that are controlled by racketeers. From its many sources of illegal revenue organized crime has a steady flow of cash with which to enter any business.

The President's Crime Commission described how organized crime infiltrates legitimate business:

Strong-arm tactics are used to enforce unfair business policy and to obtain customers. A restaurant chain controlled by organized crime used the guise of "quality control" to ensure that individual restaurant franchise-holders bought products only from other syndicate-owned businesses. In one city, every business with a particular kind of waste product useful in another line of industry sold that product to a syndicate-controlled business at one-third the price offered by legitimate business.

The cumulative effect of the infiltration of legitimate business in America cannot be measured. Law enforcement officials agree that entry into legitimate business is continually increasing and that it has not decreased organized crime's control over gambling, usury and other profitable, low-risk criminal enterprises.

Great profits are reaped by organized crime from its influence in some trade unions. Construction is a multibillion-dollar industry, and corrupt Teamsters Union leaders, linked to the mob, have forced extortionate collective bargaining agreements from real estate developers. The union has the power to slow down, expedite, or wreck any construction project. So the developers paid the price for labor peace. One investigation into New York's mob-connected cement industry found that bid rigging and overcharges added an extra $40 million to $50 million a year to building costs. That's an illegal profit that shoves already high rents even higher.

The construction of the World Trade Center in downtown New York was dominated by organized crime. An informer described how the extortion methods worked:

Those buildings could never have gone up unless our family was paid. One of the contractors was issuing four extra checks: one for Tom, Figgy, Louie Cassiano and Malpie—came to about $100,000 a year for about four years. The checks were delivered every week in Lanza's and they asked me if I wanted to be on the payroll also, but I turned it down. I was doing all right in my own business and didn't know much about this kind of stuff.

The foreman, Phillip Short, would punch the cards—punch them in in the morning and out at night. I asked Figgy why. "Well," he said, "if they don't take care of us they can't build. The Twin Towers is in our territory. They'll start putting up concrete and it gets dynamited and they have to start all over again. Their trucks won't work, metal shavings in their engines. Things like that start to happen if they don't take care of us. We control the laborers. The building gets half-way up and starts falling apart. We control the unions."

When a couple of union members began to complain about the "no shows"—men drawing paychecks without working—the mob sent Salerno and three other strong-arm men over to the job site. They rode up the elevator in an open shaft (the building had no walls yet, just the frame and the concrete floors) until they reached the eleventh floor where the two complainers were about to knock off for lunch. They forced the two men to the edge of the open elevator shaft and threatened to push them into it unless they stopped complaining about those no-show paychecks. It worked, of course.

The same Genovese crime family, according to the FBI, has dominated the Fulton Fish Market in Lower Manhattan for more than fifty years. Criminal prosecution of Mafia members for racketeering in the country's largest wholesale fish market began back in the early 1930s. But the result of this prosecution was only that different mobsters took control of the market after the previous ones went to prison. In this situation, as with many others, the federal government is now using the provisions of the 1970 Federal Racketeer Influenced and Corrupt Organizations Act, known as RICO, to smash mob control and send the criminals to prison. RICO allows the government to seize the assets of those who engage in patterns of racketeering.

In the Fulton case, U.S. attorneys claimed that members of the Genovese family had secret financial interests at the fish market and siphoned off millions of dollars yearly by extorting payments for the quick unloading and loading of perishable seafood and for allowing trucks and cars to be parked at the market, and through loan-sharking and illicit gambling. The prosecutors also charged that the principal union at the market had long been under the control of organized crime.

In recent years groups of people from other countries— Colombians, Cubans, Mexicans—have emerged as rivals to the already established crime organizations in the drug-dealing trade. One of the most dangerous criminal forces in the United States now are gangs from Jamaica. The U.S. Attorney General, Richard Thornburgh, in 1988 said there were forty separate Jamaican gangs with a total of 10,000 members operating throughout the United States. They are major traffickers of cocaine and guns, he charged, and were involved in more than 1,400 drug-related killings in the United States in the past three years. Most of the gang members are illegal aliens. The Caribbean island of Jamaica produces a potent marijuana and has been a transshipment point for cocaine. The gangs smuggle some drugs from the island into the United States and distribute them at street level.

The world heroin trade is now said to be dominated by the Triads, Chinese secret societies that developed long ago from political into massive crime organizations. They moved from mainland China to Taiwan under an alliance with Chiang Kai-shek. Their assets now mount into multi-billions of dollars from an uncontested control of the world supply of heroin. The Triads operate in cities around the world, including San Francisco and New York. Their methods, wrote Gerald Posner in his book about them, *Warlords of Crime: Chinese Secret Societies—the New Mafia,* make the Italian and the Colombian drug lords look like Boy Scouts.

It's hard to name a single illegal profit-making activity

that organized crime hasn't invaded in one way or another. It has been deeply involved in prostitution and pornography, in cargo theft, in securities theft, in the looting of union welfare and pension funds, in garbage and waste hauling, in Medicaid mills. And it can boast the largest cash haul in American history: The $5 million Lufthansa Terminal robbery at New York's Kennedy Airport in December of 1978 was pulled off by the mob.

ange Cover-Up Probed

n federal study
termine the ex-
n veterans to the
gent Orange was
celled after politi-
from the White

e sad conclusion I
n investigation and
the Subcommittee

public health experts at Columbia University and funded by the American Legion was able to use the same records to identify veterans who had been exposed to Agent Orange.

The politically-rigged CDC study has been used to dismiss new findings of health effects among Vietnam veterans that may be related to Agent Orange exposure, including reproductive disorders and certain rare forms of cancer.

The findings of the subcommittee hearing helped provide 'or legislation recently y Rep. Lane Evans (IL) utomatically compen- n veterans who have es related to Agent re. I am an original is measure, which both the Ameri- e Vietnam War

> *"The politically-rigged CDC study has been used to di___ new find'___ 'nam*

Six Guilty U. Of Stock Conspiracy

Racketeering Law Applied in Case of Princeton/Newport

By KURT EICHENWALD

euters
m, Wal.
3-year-old
ilty in Fede
es that he s
re than $10 mi
in a plea-ba
stead of investing
es, as he had pro.
buy cars, painting

ney from investors
would invest it in se-
m, who had his own
g office, said in Fed
in Manhattan.
t the money as I told
added. "Instead, I in-
d — works of art, au-
homes, and furnish-

ecurities Fraud

eaded guilty to two
d securities fraud in a
ernment.
he Federal prosecutor
Mr. Bloom would be
other charges, except
violations, unless it
he had lied to Federal

scheduled for sentenc-
Judge David N. Edel-

ho was impassive dur-
brief court appear-
eive a maximum sen-
s in jail and $500,000 i
arged twice the amoun
estors.
d to turn over all his as-
appointed receiver. The
he collected are to be
May at Sotheby's.
eter Morrison, said Mr.
operating with the re-
uld do "everything he
investors.
n said he hoped the in-
receive all their money
held out the possibility
d make a profit if the art
ell.

five principals of a defunc
investment partnership
trader with Drexel
nc. were found
ral jury in
sket

Spray, Cranberry L Is Accused of Polluting

Continued From Page A1

ocent of the charges."
he Middleboro plant manufactures company's bottled juices and its f paper containers, and packages cranberries in the fall. It dis- es about 200,000 gallons of waste a day into Middleboro's sewage ent plant, Mr. McNamara said, the largest discharger in the

dictment "should send a signal npanies, no matter how large, cannot pollute the nation's hope to pay small fines as a doing business," Mr. said. "Instead, such corpo- st understand that they rged as felons under the ironmental laws for any tions of such laws." ral law, he said, compa- t industrial waste water imit harmful emissions. nt charges that Ocean treat its acidic waste ly and that the water erry wastes and other

s. Plant Bacteria

charged that Ocean as early as October ges from its plant ia at Middleboro's works that help to minants in waste water. As the plant discharged its own treated waste into the Ne- sket River. The town has any repeated

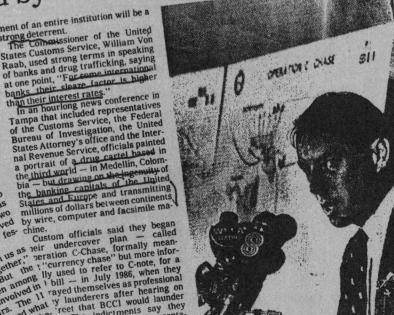

NEW HAMPSHIRE
MASSACHUSE
Boston
RHODE ISLAND
Middleboro
Miles
The New Yor

Company was charge ing pollutants throu boro sewers into Nem

Indictment sa discharges fou waste plant.

get Ocean Spray to be respo situation. Last spring, he sa asked the state environme to step in. The state got in the Federal Environmental Agency, and then the United torney entered the picture.

Pact Was Sign___
In

---

ted by U.S. in Money-Laundering

ment of an entire institution will be a strong deterrent.
The Commissioner of the United States Customs Service, William Von Raab, used strong terms in speaking of banks and drug trafficking, saying at one point, "For some international banks, their sleaze factor is higher than their interest rates."
In an hourlong news conference in Tampa that included representatives of the Customs Service, the Federal Bureau of Investigation, the United States Attorney's office and the Internal Revenue Service, officials painted a portrait of a drug cartel based in the third world — in Medellin, Colombia — but drawing on the ingenuity of the banking capitals of the United States and Europe and transmitting millions of dollars between continents by wire, computer and facsimile machine.
Custom officials said they began eir undercover plan — called peration C-Chase, formally mean- e ;"currency chase" but more infor- ad. But the ly used to refer to C-note, for a t, been among) bill — in July 1986, when they ents involved in The 11 rayed themselves as professional years. ey launderers after hearing on ney entered what reet that BCCI would launder ed to be a bache- . The indictments say they before the wedding. primarily with representa- 85 indicted were the Medellin cartel, finding i. director of camouflage the proceeds of division sales in New York City, Chi-roit, Houston, Los Angeles, Many of the

Von Raab, left, Commissioner of U. n yesterday in T

☞ 7 ☜

Crime at the Top

WHEN MOST PEOPLE think of crime they think of mugging or murder.

But what about white-collar crime?

That seems remote. Yet it has victims without number. And it costs the country far more than all the other kinds of crime added together.

What is white-collar crime? Students of crime have other terms for it: *upperworld crime, corporate crime,* or *crime at the top*. That is, crime committed by a person in a position of trust, for his or her personal gain. But it is more than the actions of such individuals who seek to achieve their goals or satisfy their needs by illegal behavior. There is also the larger aspect of organizational crime, and here we don't mean organized criminal groups like the Mafia. This is how two sociologists define it:

Organizational crimes are illegal acts of omission or comission of an individual or group of individuals in a legitimate formal organization in accordance with the operational goals of the organization, which have serious physical or economic impact on employees, consumers or the general public.

This is a rather stuffy definition, but the hard facts make its reality clear:

- Fraud by business costs the nation over $100 billion per year, reports the National Association of Attorneys General.
- Faulty goods, monopolistic practices, and other violations annually cost consumers $174 billion to $231 billion, the Senate Judiciary Committee estimates.
- When corporations violate federal regulations, taxpayers lose $10 billion to $20 billion a year, says the Department of Justice.
- In sum, the dollar cost of corporate crime in the United States is more than ten times greater than the combined total from larcenies, robberies, burglaries, and auto thefts committed by individuals.

The shock and pain and loss caused by street crime, such as robbery, are all the worse because the victim is face-to-face with the criminal. But white-collar crime can be violent, too, though the harm it does is not face-to-face. After the Ford Motor Company in the 1960s put its Pinto car on the market with defective fuel tanks, the company lost several civil suits and was indicted for reck-less homicide and criminal recklessless. In court it was revealed that Ford staffers calculated the costs of changing an unsafe gas tank would be nearly three times the ex-pected costs of suits arising because of injuries and deaths. Plainly, the company's policy and practice put profits ahead of the safety and lives of consumers.

Was this attitude something new? Way over a hundred years ago Ralph Waldo Emerson wrote in his journal: "Went to Nauset Light on the back side of Cape Cod. Collins, the keeper, told us he found obstinate resistance to the project of building a lighthouse on this coast, as it would injure the wrecking business."

It was about forty years ago that Edwin H. Sutherland published *White Collar Crime,* the first systematic study of corporate crime. By white-collar crime he meant crime committed "by persons of respectability and high social status" in the course of their work. He had examined the records of seventy of the biggest manufacturing, mining, and mercantile corporations. For sources he went to the official records of violations of laws governing restraint of trade; misrepresentation in advertising; infringement of patents, trademarks, and copyrights; unfair labor practices; illegal rebates; financial fraud; illegal conduct in wartime; and other miscellaneous offenses. None of the companies was named in his book because the publisher feared law-suits. But in 1983, in a revised edition subtitled "The Uncut Version," Yale University Press published it the way Suth-erland wrote it, with the names and case studies of the offenders included.

When the book first appeared, the average age of the

corporations described in it was forty-five years. Sutherland said that of the 70 large corporations "30 were either illegal in their origin or began illegal activities immediately after their origin." Other findings: 41 were convicted in criminal courts a total of 158 times, an average of 4 times each, a frequency that defines someone as a "habitual criminal." In addition to these convictions, a total of 822 adverse decisions were rendered against the 70, or an average of 14 adverse decisions for each of the companies.

Sutherland's research ended in 1944. Is the picture better, or worse, now? Look at the facts from authoritative sources:

- In just two years, 582 corporations surveyed in 1979 by the Justice Department racked up a total of 1,554 law violations.

- In 1980 *Fortune* magazine revealed that 11 percent of 1,043 big companies had been convicted on criminal charges or consent decrees for five offenses: bribery, criminal fraud, illegal political contributions, tax evasion, and criminal antitrust.

- In 1985, Professor Amitai Etzioni of George Washington University found that about two-thirds of the United States's five hundred largest companies were involved to some extent in illegal behavior over the preceding ten years.

It is not easy to find statistics on white-collar crime because there is no centralized reporting of corporate crime data as there is with the FBI's record of street crime.

The FBI's reports cover embezzlement, fraud, and forgery by *individuals,* but not *corporate* offenses. Why not? Why such inadequate reporting? Is it a question of priorities? Scanning the whole range of crime one sees that white-collar crime gets the least attention—perhaps because it's a less visible way of doing wrong. Yet, as Ramsey Clark pointed out:

White-collar crime is the most corrosive of all crimes. The trusted proved untrustworthy; the advantaged, dishonest. It shows the capability of people with better opportunities for creating a decent life for themselves to take property belonging to others. As no other crime, it questions our moral fiber.

To the victims the consequences of white-collar crime are often more dire than those that follow theft, burglary or robbery. White-collar crime can dig deeper than the wallet in the pocket to wipe out the savings of a lifetime. The thief takes only what is in the purse or the dresser drawer at the moment of his crime. The embezzler may reach beyond to destroy the equity of a family, ruin a whole firm, or render corporate stock valueless.

Why, then, so little moral outrage on the part of the public? Well, the injuries caused by most illegal acts of a corporation may be spread over a huge number of widely scattered victims. That is why it's better for one's public image, Professor C. Wright Mills once said, "to take one dime from each of ten million people at the point of a corporation than $100,000 from each of ten banks at the point of a gun." And, Mills added, "it is also safer."

Take pollution: It harms the body slowly, adding injury bit by bit. Price-fixing steals small amounts from a great many consumers, but most of us aren't even aware of it. It's less scary to be victimized just a little bit day after day for a very long time than to be mugged just once on the street. Add up all the small hurts and you can get an appalling sum, but who stops to think of that?

By ignoring white-collar crime we get a distorted view of the relationship between social class and crime. Since most news media stories concentrate on street crime, it gives us the impression that a great deal of serious crime is committed by the lower classes. The true picture is clouded over by the fact that official action is rarely taken against white-collar crime. Yet the facts show that all social groups, including the very rich, contain men and women with a tendency toward larceny. They are ready and willing to enlarge their income by illegal means whenever the chance appears. They like the notion of gaining more with less effort than legitimate work requires. As one expert puts it, "There is more stolen with pen and computer than by robbery face to face." Given the chance to embezzle funds from the corporation that employs him or her, why would a person burglarize a home or mug a passerby on the street?

This brings us to employee theft. "Millions of people steal billions of dollars worth of merchandise annually from the businesses and organizations where they work," according to a group of sociologists who investigate this aspect of crime. These offenders are not street criminals but "predominantly solid, respectable citizens who pay taxes, root for major league stars, believe in the 'American way of life' and the virtues of hard work and honesty, and are quickly angered by the thought of welfare chiselers, street hoodlums, and the permissiveness and immorality which they believe are upsetting an established social order."

Few of these people regard themselves as thieves, yet it is held that as many as 50 percent of the nation's work force steal from their employers. The FBI estimated that in 1973 the dollar amount they took in cash and property was $15 billion. (Compare that to $1 billion lost to street crime that same year.)

This form of crime is called embezzlement. It is theft by employees who violate their position of trust by converting their employer's money or property to their own use. They do this in many ways, ranging from the bank vice-president who pilfers his bank's money to the daily pocketing of small sums by clerks in retail stores. Few such thefts are recorded: only about 1 percent of all cases of trust violation reach the courts.

Why do so many embezzle? One reason is an urgent financial problem people believe they can solve no other way. Second, embezzlers may recognize they are in a situation where it would be easy to steal and get away with it. Third, embezzlers are able to rationalize in a way that permits them to continue to think of themselves as basically honest persons. "Honesty is the best policy," they hear all around them, "but business is business." Or, "it's all right to steal a loaf of bread when you're starving." Or they can tell themselves they are only going to use the money temporarily, so it's borrowing, not stealing. And then there are some whose troubles are so overwhelming they ask, Why am I trying to live an honest life? Where has it got me?

This aspect of wrongdoing by "business persons" includes everyone from corporate owners to blue-collar and unskilled workers.

Let's look in the next chapter at business executives who violate laws and regulations, some on behalf of their corporations, some on behalf of themselves.

Dishonest Doctor Bills Provoke New Ca...

Three common cases in which some doctors resort to insurance billing ple...

...y Finds Helmsley Guilty ...x Evasion but Not Extortion

Cosmeti
surgery
A doct
misrep
n op
llin
d Corporation

U.S. Fines Chrysler $.. Citing Workers' Expo

By JOHN HOLUSHA
Special to The New York Times

DETROIT, July 6 — The Federal | subseque...
Government today fined

Bakker and Ex-Aide Are Charged With Defrauding Donors to PT

By RONALD SMOTHERS
Special to The New York Times

CHARLOTTE, N.C., Dec. 5 — Jim
Bakker, the former leader of the PTL
television ministry, and a former top
aide were indicted today on Federal
charges of defrauding as many as
150,000 contributors and diverting
ore than $4 million for their personal
ther ministry figures were
tax evasion.
ging Mr.
as president
to a l

peals for mone
the ministry b
was short of
ing to the in
deliberately
PTL board m
tributions am
million that
tended purpo
Mr. Bakke

Executive In Fraud. In Mass

U.S. Says Ma $5 Million in

Savings Industry's Costly Fraud

By THOMAS C. HAYES
Special to The New York Times

AS, Jan. 9 — Federal regula-
mining documentation for
of multimillion-dollar
in default at insolvent sav-
utions are finding that
ore widespread than had

d in all its forms is still a
d to the collapse of the
arket in the South and
he major cause of the
y crisis, in some
egregious
tes

The abuses are 'greater than I expected,' a Texas prosecutor sa

made multimillion-dollar loans
each other's institutions, each tim
a value inflated with the help of fa
appraisals
Lately, Mr. Collins said, there ha
been discoveries of another version
d: the falsification of ne
ments by executi
institutions
ther

By LEONARD
The president of a ma
ing and bill collection co
York City was accused
frauding the Postal Se
than $5 million in po
years.
A Federal prosecutor,
said he believed the
gest fraud of its
he illegal manipu
ers and other ac
first-class postage
ieces of mail.
ccused executi
EDP Medical Co
which has of
ueens, was nam
eral indictment
racketeering,
income-tax eva
cted for mail fr
which has do
e city's Parking
other city age
pital — and
ld of Rego Park
Tied to Scanda
Maloney,
ey for the Ea

st Control Company Fined $500,000 in Death of Couple

ANOKE, Va., Nov. 17 (AP) — A
al judge fined the Orkin Extermi-
e Company $500,000 for a fumiga-
that killed a couple. The judge,
es Turk, assailed the safety prac-
at the nation's biggest pest con-
service as "scary" in their laxity
dge Turk convicted Orkin in Au-
of failing to monitor the air before
ing Hubert
their hom
e imposed
ednesday b
ose nation

An Assistant United States Attorne
Richard Pierce, said poisonous g
seeped into the mattress until the W
sons went to bed and their movemei
released the gas.

'A Tomb Sealed Up'

"That was a tomb sealed up, wait
for the occupants to enter and lay do
and die," Mr. Pierce said.
Mr. Watson, 73 years old, and his
year-old wife died days later. Expo
were killed by Vikane, wh
nate wood-boring

Hertz Concedes It Overcharged For Car Repairs

Forgeries and Bill Fraud Gained $13 Million

NYT

By RICHARD LEVINE

For seven years the Hertz Corpora-
ged motorists and insurance
es to repair cars

The Battle Against F... ...dulen

By MICHAEL deCOURCY HINDS

"Just take Dream Away before
going to bed," said the advertisement
printed in newspapers and shown on
television last year. "You will wake
up the next morning slimmer, trim-
mer and looking better than you did
before."
Should that claim have appeared in

U.S. INDICTS MAKER OF INFANTS' DRUG

Charged in

☞ 8 ☜

Profits Above People

PHONY APPLE JUICE, intended for babies?

The Beech-Nut Nutrition Corporation pleaded guilty in 1988 to 215 counts of violating federal food and drug laws. The government charged that the company had shipped mislabeled apple juice with intent to defraud and mislead the public. Millions of bottles of "apple juice" went to twenty states, Puerto Rico, the Virgin Islands, and five foreign countries. (Beech-Nut is the nation's second largest baby-food maker, after Gerber.) The product contained little or no apple juice; a Beech-Nut chemist testified it was "a chemical cocktail": sugar, water, flavoring, and coloring.

The U.S. attorney prosecuting the case said it was "a classic picture of corporate greed and irresponsibility," with the defendants' "main concern making money for Beech-Nut even if it meant selling a phony product."

Found guilty by a jury, the former chief executive and a former vice-president of Beech-Nut were sentenced to a year and a day in prison, and each was fined $100,000. The company itself agreed to pay a $2 million fine, by far the largest ever imposed in the fifty-year history of the federal Food, Drug and Cosmetic Act. Beech-Nut publicly confessed that it had broken a "sacred trust."

Of course, parents were infuriated by what Beech-Nut had done. The scandal was a demonstration of how top executives could go wrong out of blind loyalty to the corporation. In order to meet the intense competition of other baby-food makers, they were ready to violate the law. They lost sight of the babies as human beings; the juice had become merely a commodity and the baby merely a customer.

That corporate misconduct affected babies. There are many corporate crimes that destroy the environment or kill people, for example, Ford's production of the Pinto car, despite its knowledge that the gas tank was a potential bomb, waiting to be touched off when hit by another vehicle from the rear. It would have cost only $11 to make each car safe, but the corporation decided against the change. Hundreds of people were killed or injured.

In the 1960s Ford made another faulty car whose transmission could slip from park to reverse; if that happened, it triggered the release of the parking brake, which meant the car could run into whatever was in its path, perhaps a person. It would have cost only a few cents per car to make design changes to correct the problem, but the company failed to do it. By the time it stopped making that transmission in 1980, more than four hundred people had been killed and thousands injured by runaway Fords.

If these numbers of needless deaths and injuries are appalling, what can be said about the world's worst industrial disaster? It happened soon after midnight on December 3, 1984, when an accident resulted in a leak of gas from a pesticide factory in Bhopal, India, controlled by the American firm Union Carbide. The gas poured across the city of 800,000 people. About 1,700 people died within hours of the leak, with the toll rising to 3,500 by the end of 1988. Up to 200,000 people were injured in the accident. Doctors said many of these will die and others will become too sick to work. Some 30,000 to 40,000 people suffered serious damage to eyes, lungs, and brains.

Union Carbide officials had learned before the accident that the plant had many defective instruments and "safety" valves, that its labor force was poorly trained, and that its management was negligent. A secret report given the company by a team of experts warned that the plant had "serious potential for sizable releases of toxic materials." In the years preceding the gas leak there had been six serious accidents at the plant, but Union Carbide did nothing to check the quality of the plant's operation. And then the disaster struck.

If lawsuits for damages had been filed in American courts, the company could have been swamped. But a federal judge transferred the lawsuits to courts in India. Unequipped to handle such a huge legal burden, the courts took a long time to settle the claims. Early in 1989, though, the Indian government made a claim of $3 billion against

Union Carbide. India's Supreme Court ordered the corporation to pay $470 million in damages for the gas leak. Union Carbide accepted the ruling. The court did not fix blame for the disaster. The press noted that the settlement would have "only a small financial impact on Carbide."

A grim heritage from the war in Vietnam is the damage done by Agent Orange. It was a defoliant, a chemical applied to plants to make their leaves fall off. Agent Orange's chemical contents were known by the maker, Dow Chemical, to be extremely hazardous. Just three ounces, if placed in New York City's water supply, could wipe out the city's entire population. Yet 130 pounds of the dioxin were scattered over Vietnam—on civilians as well as the military.

The Pentagon had ordered quantities of Agent Orange sprayed to kill vegetation in the combat zone so that the enemy would find it hard to hide. Apparently the corporation and the six other companies that contributed to the sale did not warn the Pentagon of the danger of Agent Orange. Nor were the troops who did the spraying or moved through that area warned. Returning veterans by the thousands found themselves suffering from a variety of physical ailments, and some of their children were born with severe birth defects.

When many lawsuits were filed for damages by thousands of veterans and their survivors in 1978, Dow and the other companies settled out of court for $180 million, but with interest the fund has grown to $240 million. The agreement was protested by the veterans. They thought it pin money for a corporation that grosses some $10 billion a year. (And that payment was largely covered by insurance.)

At most, veterans injured by the herbicide can expect to receive $12,600 each, with the average payment about $5,700. Would such a sum compensate Vietnam veteran Michael Ryan and his wife Maureen, whose first daughter was born with no rectum, no urethra, two vaginas, four ovaries, minus one elbow and one wrist, and with spine and muscle problems, limp arm, missing fingers, a hole in the heart, and two cervixes?

In 1989 millionaire Leona Helmsley was convicted of evading $1.2 million in federal income taxes. She and her husband had built a large house and charged such luxuries as a marble dance floor above a swimming pool, a $45,000 silver clock, and a $130,000 stereo system to their hotel and real estate empire.

Tax *evasion* is what the Helmsleys were charged with, and it is a criminal offense, punishable by big fines and jail terms. Tax *avoidance*, however, is not a crime. It is legal to try to organize your affairs to keep your taxes as low as possible.

But not everyone has equal opportunity to avoid taxes. The tax laws and regulations are so complex that it takes high-priced lawyers and accountants to find and exploit all the loopholes. The borderline between legitimate minimizing and illegal manipulating is very vague. Corporations are best equipped to walk the tightrope. "Taxes," one expert writes, "are now the motivating factor in thousands of business maneuvers." So common are violations of the tax laws by business that statisticians estimate that if everyone liable to income tax made honest payment, it would enable the government to decrease the general tax burden by 40 percent.

Tax criminals commonly tell themselves nobody is really hurt by their conduct; it's only the government that is the victim. That easy form of self-deception ignores the largely unrecognized fact that the individual citizen pays heavily for what the corporate criminal does. It costs the country, according to one estimate, $100 billion yearly in lost taxes because of unreported income.

But there are some areas where the social costs of white-collar crime are widely recognized. More than once, congressional investigations have exposed illegal price-fixing by the American drug industry, causing excessively high prices to the sick and bringing excessively high profits to the corporations. Misleading drug advertising has also been laid to the industry. Even more important are violations of regulations set forth by the federal Food and Drug Administration (FDA). Consider the dangers to the public of the release on the market of new and inadequately tested drugs, as well as drugs known to have harmful effects or side effects about which the consumer is not properly warned.

How does it happen that we continue to drink polluted water, breathe poisoned air, ride in unsafe automobiles, swallow harmful medicine? None of these hazards to our health and safety is legally permissible. Through a multitude of regulatory statutes, the law is supposed to protect us. But the law is not enforced. In 1968, the president's *Crime Commission Report* said:

The crucial fact is that these laws are violated on a vast scale, sometimes in deliberate disregard of the law, sometimes because businessmen, in their effort to come as close to the line between legality and illegality as possible, overstep it.

Enforcing the laws against white collar crime is not an easy thing to do under these circumstances. How many elected officials will urge a district attorney to arrest property owners or corporate managers who violate housing codes, air and water pollution laws, or health and safety standards? That some do, is a tribute to their independence. Robert Morgenthau, Manhattan district attorney, pointed out to a national meeting of industry leaders the problem of "persons who publicly denounce crimes of violence while privately committing more 'socially acceptable' white collar crimes."

Yet these "acceptable" crimes cause huge damage to untold numbers of human beings. In 1988, expert witnesses told the Senate Labor Committee that 50,000 to 70,000 workers were dying of occupational diseases each year because the Reagan administration had delayed new federal health regulations and had not enforced existing standards. Another 350,000 workers incurred illnesses each year because of inactivity by the Occupational Safety and Health Administration (OSHA).

One of the largest fines ever imposed for violating job health and safety regulations—$1.5 million—was levied against the Chrysler Corporation in 1987. The company agreed to pay the fine for 811 violations, including willfully exposing workers to lead and arsenic. "Willful" means that Chrysler knew of the shortcomings but did not correct them.

An even bigger fine—$4.3 million—was imposed by OSHA on John Morell & Company in 1988 for hundreds of "egregious" and "willful" violations at the meat-packer's plant in Sioux Falls, South Dakota. The government agency said Morrell ignored workplace hazards that allowed 880 of its 2,000 employees to suffer serious, sometimes disabling, muscular injuries.

In another case a drug maker and its distributor were indicted by a federal grand jury for misrepresenting the safety and effectiveness of a drug used in treating premature infants. The government reported that thirty-eight infants had died of symptoms associated with the drug's use.

Indifference to law can take odd forms. Two overnight cargo delivery companies were accused by the Justice Department in 1988 of operating thousands of illegal cargo plane flights for a five-year period and were charged with pressuring pilots to fly in unsafe weather and when planes were overweight or improperly loaded. In the still-pending case, the companies, involved in four fatal plane crashes, reportedly flew twenty-two flights a night out of a New Jersey airport, without holding a proper government license. When seeking business, the companies were said to have told customers they were certified airlines when in fact they were not. They could underbid competitors because they didn't have the high expense of complying with the rules. The U.S. attorney accused them of grabbing for profits without heed to the crucial goal of air safety.

Industry tends to resist attempts to control such harmful practices. It was only Upton Sinclair's exposure of terrible conditions in the meat-packing industry in his book *The Jungle* that brought about the Pure Food and Drug Act of 1906, the first major control bill. Not until 1938 was the Food and Drug Administration (FDA) set up to test and control the introduction of new drugs. And this too came about as the result of a hundred deaths from the premature marketing of a new drug. Another law strengthening control by the FDA was adopted in 1962. It came about after the thalidomide horror, when thousands of babies were born deformed because their mothers had taken the tranquilizer thalidomide early in pregnancy.

Medical fraud extends beyond what the giant and "respectable" companies have sometimes been charged with. It covers a wide range of illicit practices by the smaller, sometimes individual operators who offer "miracle" medicines and quack remedies touted to cure everything from cancer and heart disease to sexual impotence. Untold numbers of people desperately searching for a new way out of their health problems are deceived by ruthless entrepreneurs.

In recent years many physicians have been convicted of faking private insurance or Medicare and Medicaid claims. They have listed patients who don't exist or treatments that were never given, to increase the payment they or their patients receive. The Aetna insurance company estimated that fraud by physicians, dentists, chiropractors, and podiatrists cost more than $10 billion a year.

The car repair industry is notorious for fraudulent practices. In 1988 the Hertz Corporation admitted that for seven years it had been charging motorists and insurance companies higher prices to repair cars damaged in accidents than it actually paid. The company estimated it had collected $13 million through questionable billing, forgery, and other deceptive practices.

Listing of such criminal acts could go on and on. Here are just a few taken from recent press accounts:

- A former official of Intelsat, a satellite consortium, pleaded guilty of scheming to obtain $4.8 million by fraudulent means.

- A federal investigation of fraudulent transactions in the Texas savings industry disclosed that executives had falsified documents, taken kickbacks on loans, misused funds, and made false statements to federal regulators. A similar investigation in California revealed that the Lincoln Savings and Loan Association had been milked by its chairman, Charles A. Keating, Jr., of $34 million which went to himself and family members in the few years before its demise.

- A former PaineWebber vice-president was sentenced to six months in jail and fined $510,000 for a money-laundering scheme. He pleaded guilty to helping customers of his Wall Street firm hide huge investments from the government.

- A Northwestern University professor of obstetrics and gynecology was indicted on charges of perjury and obstructing justice in the testimony he gave for A. H. Robins, the maker of the Dalkon Shield, an intrauterine birth-control device. He had said the device was not unreasonably dangerous and that his finding was based in part on experiments conducted under his supervision. Later he admitted he had not conducted the experiments. The company had paid him $277,000 for witness and consulting fees over a five-year period. About 200,000 users of the device are pressing claims against the company for serious injuries because of the intrauterine device. It is one of the largest mass-injury cases in history.

Almost from the beginning the company's executives knew the Dalkon Shield was ineffective and a health hazard. They consistently denied having any knowledge of its dangers, but the evidence produced in the course of the lawsuits against Robins showed that the company deliberately suppressed the information. Not until 1984—a year after it began to market the device—did Robins consent to a notice recalling all Dalkon Shields still in use.

- In 1988, a federal jury in New Jersey found that a cigarette manufacturer, the Liggett Group, was liable in a woman's death from lung cancer. It was the first time a tobacco company lost a claim. The woman's husband was awarded $400,000 because the jury decided that the company had failed to warn of the health hazard in smoking before 1966 (when warnings were not required on cigarette packs).

In his book, *Merchants of Death: The American Tobacco Industry,* Larry C. White pointed out that smoking killed more Americans in 1986 (over 350,000) than died in World War II. Cigarettes cost the nation more than $50 billion in health care and lost salaries that year, while the industry made billions in profits.

- Suffolk County in New York State accused the Long Island Lighting Company of repeatedly lying and of filing false documents with regulatory commissions in its efforts to complete the Shoreham nuclear power plant. Increases in rates as a result of the fraud amounted to an estimated $2.9 billion, the county claimed.

- The president of a major mass marketing and bill collection company in New York was accused of defrauding the U.S. Postal Service of $5 million in postage over ten years. He was charged with racketeering, mail fraud, bribery, and income tax evasion.

- The federal government charged an international bank holding company of a conspiracy with cocaine dealers to launder millions of dollars in illegal drug money. BCCI, the holding company, was said to have assets of about $20 billion and offices in seventy countries. Bank officials had been involved in previous cases, but this was the first time a bank itself was indicted for laundering money.

- The president of a small manufacturing company in Pennsylvania was sentenced to a fifteen-year prison term for defrauding the government. His crime was slipping inferior materials into equipment for fighting fires aboard naval vessels when they were at sea and using defective procedures to make the equipment.

Most of the crimes listed here were committed by company executives. In a study called *Corporate Crime and Violence,* the author, Russell Mokhiber, points out that the largest robbery in American history totaled $5.4 million. But the far larger cost of white-collar crime has recently been estimated by a Senate subcommittee to be between $174 billion and $231 billion annually. One company after another has been shown to place short-term profits far above human life, community safety, or the long-term health of the environment.

STLE-BLOWERS
IN BUSH BACKING

uilty Pleas in Pentagon Fraud

By MICHAEL WINES

Special to The New York Times

ANDRIA, Va., Sept. 26 —
en and a Los Angeles-based
pleaded guilty to-

ident, in a Compromise,
grees to Reverse Reagan
and Support Measure

2 Sentenced
In Pentagon
Bribery Case

Family Rises
Using Fraud
On Medicaid

By SUSAN F. RASKY
Special to The New York Times
INGTON, March 7 — P

By SELWYN RAAB

Sheldon Weinberg owned a modest
shop in Brooklyn before he and his
branched off into Medicaid ventures.
new business quickly brought them t
ish trappings of success: six-fig
comes, a yacht, a $100,000 Rolls
apartments in Trump Tower, a
maid and a $2.5 million home in Flor

orkers Who Turn In Bosses
se Law to Seek Big Rewards

But that wealth, prosecutors s
hardly created by the delivery of
services to poor people, but by a $1
fraud, the largest theft of Medica
officials say, since the program
years ago.

By RICHARD W. STEVENSON

Five Years After Settleme
Agent Orange War Lives

ANGELES, July 9 —
ustice Department
settled charges that
ntractor had overch
e Force and the Nav
rings, there were tw

The Weinbergs, the prosecutors
ated a sophisticated computeri
of fraud that included the sub
381,000 fake claims to the sta
ments of $5,000 a week to a den
the scheme. One son was said t
part of one clinic as an office for
ty-trading business.

Government recoy
million from the comp
al Tectonics, of De
and a former Tecto
ee who had started
1985 by filing a civil l
ing out evidence of
rging won a $1.4 mill

By STEPHEN LABATON

Five years after the $180 million
settlement in the case brought by
thousands of Vietnam veterans and
their survivors against the makers of
the herbicide Agent Orange, the outcome of the complex civil case is still
being criticized by veterans and un-
dergoing scrutiny by the legal community.

Many veterans, who hav
tributed birth defects, cancer
other illnesses to exposure to t
foliant Agent Orange, view the
tion as a symbol of their mis
ment by society and the Governl

Tomorrow, Mr. Weinberg,
and his sons, Jay, 35, and Rona
sentenced in State Supreme C
lyn for the fraud, which to
even years at clinics in the B
nt and Bushwick sections of

ase marked the larg
recovery in recent yea
nce-moribund provisio
ederal False Claims A

"You can't in all honesty say
the legal system worked — it ha
said Frank McCarthy, a veter
Orlando, Fla., who has been inv
izing veterans since the
"It has destroyed
system for
ets in

Roller-Coaster Rise

A portrait of the We
coaster financial rise and
family strife, emerged from
documents and from interv
and former business assoc

Since the landmark settlement was
reached five years ago yesterday,
about $3 million — less than 2 percent
the fund — has gone to veterans
and many of thos
een made in recer
because of lef
inistrative snags
tters. At most,
the herbicide ca
$12,600 each,
ive years.
more than $20
gone to plaint
appointed offi
ts and the con
the vetera
ls show.
millions of d
actors have
re diligent
es. They a
aw has pro
artment

New Delay
Is Seen for
Bomber

MILITARY SUPPLIER
FINED $115 MILLION
ON FRAUD CHARGES

men. The Weinbergs, thro
declined to be interviewed

The portrait showed a
pervisory agencies to c
operation and detect the
questions about the lice
ing of large outpatient
run by investors witho

Northrop Accused of
1 Billion Overbilling

SETTLEMENT SETS RECORD

Sundstrand Admits P
to Overbill the P
by Million

fect
awye
the cas

Charles A. Grassley, an
Representative John D. Dingell
crat, said they provided evidenc
the Defense and Justice Depart
eral, responded that the cur
perfect example of how the
cause when that informati
ion is combined from the
and aggressive action
inquiry began a
ficial report
ed by

By ANDREA ADELSON
Special to The New York Times
S ANGELES, Feb. 25 — N
es of financial impropr
orthrop Corporation r
rther delay of the
cret Stealth b
financial
y contr
Ar

ntagon: Was Someone

ce of this earth that
or — greed. And
een work-
stiga-
of

Pentagon Official Accu
8 Concerns on Secret Da

"But there is no system c
completely obviates the
that is why we have po
The Pentagon. In the
ing harder. In the
tions by the insp
Defense resulte

By RICHARD HALLORAN
Special to The New York Times

By JOHN H. CUSHMAN Jr.

WASHINGTON
N before the current Federal investigation
bery and fraud in military contract-
light, there was plenty of evi-
ide abuses of the system.
lf of the Pentagon's
vestigation for

WASHINGTON, Dec. 21 — The
director of a Defense Department
investigative agency said today
that eight of the nation's leading
arms makers face possible criminal prosecution for illegal
ssion of secret Gove
ments

ndictments, ac
During the p
tions and
volved p
sions a
fold s

separate from the Justice D
ment's well-publicized
into possible impropri
consultants to

☞ 9 ☜

The Pentagon:
A Honey Pot

THE LARGEST centrally managed economy in the world (outside the Soviet Union) is run by the U.S. Defense Department, or the Pentagon, as its headquarters building is called. For comparison, note that the Pentagon's budget for 1989 was $294 billion, a sum about ten times greater than the gross national product of Greece or Egypt, six times greater than South Africa's, almost twice as big as Mexico's.

Plainly, there is ample opportunity for white-collar crime within so huge an enterprise dealing in billions. In 1988, the press headlined federal investigations of large-scale fraud and bribery in military contracting. Pentagon officials making contracts with corporations producing military equipment were allegedly accepting payments from them or their consultants in exchange for confidential information on government contracts.

The FBI described one scheme involving the McDonnell Douglas Corporation, the nation's largest military contractor, and a prominent consultant. The consultant who worked with the corporation was a former senior official with the U.S. Navy. The information the company got from the consultant could provide it with an unfair advantage over its competitors and/or the government.

The charges reflected the "classic revolving door syndrome" in Washington, D.C., where senior officials of the military leave their posts and become private consultants to the military contractors they have long done business with. Reportedly some make improper use of information, much of it classified, obtained during their government service. It helps the contractors obtain Defense Department contracts worth tens of millions of dollars. Such information could include details about contract bids of rival companies.

In the McDonnell Douglas case, the FBI said several federal laws might have been broken, including bribery of public officials, theft of government property, and conspiracy to defraud the United States.

Overbilling is another example of white-collar crime in the defense system. One major military contractor, the Northrop Corporation, was charged with overbilling the federal government by at least $1 billion for work done on the secret Stealth bomber. The charge came from lawsuits filed by former and current employees of Northrop. The U.S. Air Force planned to buy 132 of the Stealth bombers at a cost of $37 billion. Still other such employees filed suits contending that the company made false claims on its work on the guidance systems of the MX missile.

Another such case resulted from a four-year grand jury investigation of TRW Inc. The company pleaded guilty to federal charges of conspiracy to overcharge the government on contracts involving military aircraft and parts for the M-1 tank. The overcharges totaled millions of dollars in what the U.S. attorney called a conspiracy "to defraud the U.S." and to "enrich TRW."

As a result of repeated exposures of such offenses, an industry-wide program was aimed at encouraging voluntary disclosure of wrongdoing. Under the program, thirty-four of the top hundred military contractors had disclosed possibly fraudulent practices by mid-1988. Before 1988 was over, more than four thousand people, most of them in uniform, were convicted of misdeeds involving contracting.

Some of the most brazen contract violations ever encountered in an investigation of a corporation doing business with the Pentagon came to light when the Sundstrand Corporation agreed to pay fines and penalties totaling $115 million. The Illinois aerospace company admitted to a conspiracy to overcharge the government on military contracts. Sundstrand, said the Justice Department, went far beyond overcharging the government for cost overruns. It also handed in false bills for executive expenses such as household servants, nonbusiness travel, country club dues, liquor, baby-sitters, jewelry, saunas, lobbying costs, dog kennels, gifts, cigarettes, candy, radar detectors, and snow-plowing at the homes of company officials.

Nearly half of all contracts involved in a four-year investigation of the defense industry were found to be overpriced. Hundreds of millions of dollars of excess charges by dozens of contractors were discovered by auditors. One senator said that "there is an attitude with the defense industry of 'catch us if you can' and we've got to change that ethic to 'we'll catch you if you do.' "

To meet the problem, Congress began to consider protective measures: more money to pay for investigators and attorneys to prosecute fraud by military contractors; increased fines; extension of the statute of limitations; rewards for whistle-blowers who provide evidence of wrongdoing; an increase in the number of auditors who visit contractors' plants looking for evidence of overbilling.

Ironically, some of the weapons that were bought at extravagant cost to the government and that brought superprofits to the corporations don't work. The army's Bradley troop carrier, said weapons experts, would risk sinking if it tried to cross deep water and streams during combat. The fleet of AH64 helicopters the army bought was discovered to have cracks in the rotor blades. The fleet had to be grounded.

Yet the military contracts continue to draw huge profits from the government. The government's General Accounting Office, a watchdog agency, reported that profits pocketed by the defense industry during the Reagan administration's $1.5 trillion defense buildup were 12 percent greater than those earned by nondefense commercial firms.

The very nature of what President Dwight D. Eisenhower called the "military industrial complex" makes rip-offs not only possible but likely. Corporations, so the general public believes, are business enterprises separate from the government. But the distinction disappears, especially when companies like Lockheed do most of their business with government. They make use of government-owned plants and of capital supplied by government. Their unplanned extra costs are taken care of by the government, and if they get into a disastrous financial situation, as Lockheed once did, they are rescued by the government.

Under such an arrangement, there are basic reasons why white-collar crimes are committed and overlooked in the defense industry. One is that the details of defense contracts are concealed behind the screen of "national security." Mustn't ask too many questions! Another is that arms contracts are often not awarded competitively. Defense officials ask Congress to trust them, on deals that may be worth hundreds of billions of dollars. How then can the taxpaying public be sure it is not being ripped off? Then there is the cost-plus arrangement. The contract assures the company a profit figured as a percentage of the company's costs. So if management makes serious mistakes or is inefficient, it doesn't absorb the cost overrun. The government picks up the tab.

Everyone has heard of at least some examples of the mess in military procurement. The Pentagon bought a $7,622 coffee brewer, a $659 plastic ashtray, a $35 hammer. It paid $9,609 for a 12¢ wrench, $387 for a $3 flat washer, $27 for a 9¢ screw, $258 for a $1.69 Phillips screwdriver. It stockpiled boots that did not fit the needs of men in combat.

Corruption? For years complaints were made by whistleblowers—angry government officials, defense auditors, even company employees. But nothing happened until the scandals erupted in 1988 and the administration and Congress began to act.

In a very different kind of case, though still involving the government's role in defense, major liability lawsuits are being filed by employees and neighbors of the nation's nuclear weapons plants. These are the responsibility of the U.S. Department of Energy. Some 14,000 plaintiffs joined in a suit over radiation leakage at a weapons plant in Fernald, Ohio. They believe that they were exposed to injury from radiation leaks. Government officials have admitted accidents, leaks of radioactive gases, and severe mismanagement of nuclear waste programs in the nation's nuclear bomb production complex. It includes seventeen major facilities in twelve states. For the past four decades nuclear weapon production has polluted the air, soil, and water in these plants and research laboratories. The contaminants include uranium, plutonium, cesium, strontium, PCBs, chromium, arsenic, mercury, and solvents used in making nuclear weapons. The people suing believe they have developed cancer, blood disorders, unexplained illnesses, and other problems, because of the plants. The operators of the bomb plants knew years ago that there were critical structural flaws and deficiencies in management and maintenance, according to the Energy Department.

The plant contractors include large corporations like Western Electric, E. I. DuPont de Nemours & Co., and Rockwell International Corporation. The people who consider themselves victims believe they were deceived by the government about the risks of the highly secret bomb plants. But experts on such litigation say the government and its military contractors are protected by legal rules that make it "nearly impossible for people to win suits based on lapses at the weapons complex." The people who have been injured are fighting giant corporations with the resources to resist such damage suits, and the federal government has indicated it will aggressively fight the nuclear damage cases.

BOESKY SENTENCED TO 3 YEARS

x-Morgan Analyst Is Sentenced to 3-Year Prison

illegal tradin
Wang more sp
men also sp
amount of n
to $1 million

Mr. Wang, 24 years old, showed little emotion as Federal District Judge Kevin T. Duffy harshly lectured him before passing sentence.

amends for it."
The charges filed by the United States Attorney in Manhattan accused Mr. Wang of engaging in two

Mr. Lee
count each
charg

By KURT EICHENWALD

tephen Sui-Kuan Wang Jr., a former junior analyst with Morgan Stanley & Co nv. was sentenced yesterday ears in sider tradison f g sch her p

'You Blew It on Greed'

"You had a brilliant fu blew it on greed," Judg "You had practically ociety could give you. st society place could

was the subject of and Ex-

Trader's Plea Reveals New
In Battle on Wall St. Cor

By KURT EICHENWALD

plead guilty to one cha to commit securities fr lating the prices of at l for up to two years p 1987.

Government officials nian's plea was the f criminal inquiry into sh the securities markets d 1987 collapse.

Officials in the United ney's office in Manhattan eral Bureau of Investiga resources and manpower verted since the crash n tions of apparent illegal a

Mr. gan ion plo mc fr

New York Mounts Campaign
Against Wall St. Tax Cheats

Several Federal

agencies have tigation of stock evidence that lt of the market 87, officials re-

arks a new front crackdown on n, which began in publicly identified nsider trading and inquiry, which in-number of firms, these well-known

By ELIZABETH KOLBERT
Special to The New York Times

ALBANY, Oct. 17 — As part of a major drive against income-tax evasion by Wall Street brokers and investment house employees, the state tax department announced today that it would withhold taxes from bonuses and commissions at the state's highest rate starting Jan. l.

The move follows the department's cent discovery that at least 15,000 all Street employees appeared to ve filed no state income tax returns at least one of the last three years. hose employees, many making b ries, are paying withholdin hey probably have not — nt they owe, espe bonuses, tax

Later this week the department plans to notify 5,000 more Wall Street employees that they, too, owe the state tax returns. And next week the depart-ment plans to send out another 5,000 letters.

Tax officials said they had found so many employees who d not filed re-turns that they w those with t later in with

igation came to light e announcement by ni, the United States hattan, that Stanley mer president of a rities firm, the Haas at a ration, agreed to taxes on Wall ts on at y belie

'Task Force Without a

Over the last year, m F.B.I. agents in the New have been trained by the Se Exchange Commission t market manipulation, and ined throughout tl

ll St. 'Whiz Kid' Gets
3-Year Term for Fraud

By ARNOLD H. LUBASCH

avid P. Bloom, a financial adviser e characterized as a Wall Street niz kid, was sentenced yesterday to ght years in prison for defrauding in-estors of almost $15 million. imposing the sentence — an un-ong one for an investment David N. Edelstein as a ar-old defendant was tors. "I find es, com- ge

to two fraud charges, each carrying a sentence of up to five years. The judge sentenced him to four years on each charge and made the sentences consec-utive.

Art, Homes and C

Mr. Bloom displayed li but he seemed to swallo the judge said the two se be served consecutively. Mr. Bloom, a 1985 D graduate, was accused investors, many of ther parents, by taking th ding to make in used

sky di now Bar,

Trader's Plea Reveal
In Battle on Wall S

By KURT EICHENWA

ncies have tion of stock lence that he market icials re-

plead guil to commit lating the for up to 1987.

Governm nian's plea criminal inq the securiti 1987 collapse.

Officials in ney's office in eral Bureau of resources and verted since th tions of apparen

'Task Force

Over the last F.B.I. agents in ave been trained xchange Comm rket manipulat trained throu James C. E ant director o ffice.

e agents hav year with Mr ribed yester out a name

'JUNK BOND' LEADER
IS INDICTED BY U.S.
IN CRIMINAL ACTION

MILKEN FACES 98 COUNTS

Forfeitures of $1.8 Billion Are
Asked From Drexel Expert
and 2 Others at Firm

By STEPHEN LABATON

In the largest criminal action against a Wall Street figure, a Federal grand jury today indicted Michael R. Milken, the Drexel Burnham Lambert Inc. ex-ecutive who transformed corporate lawyer, takeovers through the pioneering use ge tha of high-yield "junk bonds." prepos Prosecutors said they would seek an to be unprecedented financial penalty m owed against individuals, totaling $1.8 billion re and in forfeitures from Mr. Milken and two s and re in charges from a name in the

rexel Guilty Plea Expecte
Fraud Case on Monday

y STEPHEN LABATON

el Burnham Lambert Inc. will guilty plea on Monday to six counts of mail and securities eople in the United States At-office and at the investment d yesterday.

ility plea would end eight of negotiations and appeals plea-bargain agreement, disclosed in December. As settlement, the investment agreed to pay fines and res-$650 million. In a related with the Securities and Commission, it has under-restructuring

eral Judge Milton Pollack in the S.E.C. action against Drexel. Earlier this summer, the Supreme Court de-clined to hear that challenge.

Lawyers for the Milkens had also intervened in the criminal case against Drexel, asserting that the plea agreement between the firm and the Government had unfairly blocked the Milkens from receiving their 1988 compensation.

That challenge was recently with-drawn, after an agreement the law-yers reached with prosecutors late last month to drop a provision that re-quired Drexel to withhold compensa-tion owed to the Mil-

☞ 10 ☜

Greed on Wall Street

"GREED IS a nice religion," said the professor. "If you are really greedy, you are going to keep your shoes polished, you won't run around on your wife or get drunk. You will do whatever it takes to maximize your lifetime income, and that doesn't leave time for messing up." This was Dennis Levine's favorite professor talking, preaching a sermon on the virtues of avarice to a class of business majors. When Levine graduated, he entered banking as a management trainee and soon moved on up to investment banking.

The first of his family to attend college, Levine felt like an outsider among the Ivy League types who dominated Wall Street. Burning to prove himself smarter than his colleagues, he opened a Swiss bank account and began playing the stock market with insider information. He used tips from lawyers, investment bankers, and others who knew about likely corporate takeovers before they were publicly announced. For five years his scheme worked smoothly. He reaped profits of $12.6 million from an original investment of $170,000, shifting from one investment banking firm to another and ending up at Drexel Burnham Lambert, Inc.

In May 1986, he was arrested for making illegal profits from insider trading. But young Mr. Levine did not repent his sins. "This is the biggest insider trading scandal in history," he bragged, "and it's all because of me." He was not done with trading: in exchange for the prospect of a lighter prison sentence he informed on his conspirators. A federal judge sentenced him to two years in prison on charges of securities fraud, tax fraud, and perjury. He was also fined $362,000 and returned $11.6 million in illegal profits.

His scam went as far as it did because Levine's co-workers and clients looked the other way. Some who knew him were aware that the millions he raked in were not the result of brilliance as a stock analyst but the outcome of his ability to use illegally the information he acquired. Levine's professor proved to be wrong: greed creates lots of chances to make a mess.

Greed is basic to the white-collar criminal's aim in life, said Rudolph W. Giuliani, the U.S. attorney who prosecuted many of these criminals. But once they pile up lots of money, white-collar criminals want celebrity—recognition from their felonious peers. This motivation is different from gun-toting criminals. They want to make a

name for themselves, to be the best—or is it the worst?—
in their own line of work. It is a matter of power and pride.
For white-collar criminals, going to prison is shameful
because they lose their standing among friends. To be
caught red-handed means they weren't that smart in the
first place.

Because of Dennis Levine's informing, Ivan Boesky, one
of the financial world's most powerful speculators, was also
trapped. Boesky was charged with illegally earning more
than $50 million by trading with insider information he
bought from Levine. Boesky then disclosed that he addi-
tionally earned more than $30 million by trading with
inside information sold to him for $700,000 by Martin A.
Siegel, once one of Wall Street's top corporate merger
specialists. Siegel pleaded guilty to criminal charges. An
intricate web of criminal connections spun out from these
men to entangle other individuals and companies.

Boesky settled civil insider trading charges by paying a
record $100 million. He was sentenced to three years in
prison for conspiring to file false stock trading records.
The case, said the government, underscored both the enor-
mity of Boesky's crimes and the unimagined scope of the
corruption in Wall Street. Federal District Judge Morris
E. Lasker, who sentenced him, emphasized that a prison
term was necessary to try to stanch what he charged was
a widespread disregard for the law:

Recent history has shown that the kind of erosion of morals
and standards and obedience to the law involved in such a case
as this is unhappily widespread in both business and govern-

ment. The time has come when it is totally unacceptable for courts to act as if prison is unthinkable for white-collar defendants but a matter of routine in other cases. Breaking the law is breaking the law.

The maximum penalty Boesky had faced was a five-year sentence. Some observers felt the three years he got was on the low side. Boesky, a lawyer born in Detroit, was, according to the *New York Times,* "a model of the riches that the takeover frenzy of the last decade had delivered into the hands of nimble investors known as arbitragers, who made their living trading stocks of companies involved in or rumored to be the subject of takeovers." He was said to have been worth several hundred million dollars. He rode in limousines, owned a luxury apartment in Manhattan and, a huge estate in Westchester county, and made handsome donations to philanthropies.

When Levine led the authorities to him, Boesky agreed to plead guilty and cooperate with the government. He secretly tape-recorded conversations with his alleged confederates to gain evidence incriminating them. The U.S. attorney's office said that the cases involving Boesky and others "revealed that criminal conduct is at the heart of a substantial amount of market activity by established securities industry professionals."

In the wake of the Boesky case, vast securities fraud and insider trading charges were filed against Drexel Burnham Lambert, Inc., by the Securities and Exchange Commission (SEC) in 1988. In summary, Drexel and several of its top executives were charged with engineering a two-year scheme to violate the securities laws, defraud Drexel customers, trade on inside information, and manipulate the prices of stock. As part of that arrangement, Boesky acted as a "front" for Drexel. Following the SEC charges against Drexel, the U.S. attorney's office said it was investigating Drexel for a broad pattern of criminal activity including racketeering.

Faced with fraud charges, Drexel unleashed an arsenal of image-building weapons. A huge and costly public relations campaign was initiated to make the public think well of Drexel and to help the defense lawyers representing the firm. Not much needed to be done in the financial district, apparently, as the *New York Times* headlined, "Wall Street Unruffled by Drexel Case."

Reporters combed the financial district for reactions to the pending indictments. Typical of the response was what Henry R. Kravis, a Drexel client, said. He "privately voiced some discomfort" but would, nevertheless, retain Drexel's services "because of its ability to get the deal done." Following the story day after day, one could find not a single denunciation of Drexel executives for wrongdoing by any Wall Streeter.

The SEC suit offered an insight into why clients were staying with the firm. Drexel's reported misdeeds actually benefited some of them. Why bite the hand that feeds you?

There was plenty of work to do as the U.S. attorney's office in New York tried to clean up the mess on Wall Street. Here are a few examples of the results of their investigations:

- Stephen Sui-Kuan Jr., 24, was sentenced to three years in federal prison for his part in an insider trading scheme. The former junior analyst for Morgan Stanley & Co. worked on mergers and acquisitions. In passing sentence Judge Kevin Duffy said: "You had a brilliant future and you blew it on greed. You had practically every break society could give you. You breached the trust society placed in you. The first time you could have been a crook, you were."

- William Dillon, 34, a discharged Merrill Lynch & Co. stockbroker, pleaded guilty to fraud. He had traded securities based on a stock-touting column in *Business Week* magazine, copies of which he bought in advance of publication from a worker in the printing plant.

- Peter N. Brant, 35, the former top retail stockbroker at Kidder Peabody & Co., was sentenced to eight months in prison for trading stocks, using inside information about forthcoming articles in the *Wall Street Journal*. His sentence was relatively light because he gave information to the government about other people in the scheme. Brant's commission income had been about $2 million. He owned a million-dollar estate on Long Island and a $2 million co-op apartment in Manhattan. His conspiracy had taken in about $690,000.

- Robert A. Rough, 49, a former director of the Federal Reserve Board of New York, was indicted on insider trading charges, accused of leaking information on interest rate policy to a New Jersey securities firm. The information he provided was said to enable the firm fraudulently to make millions of dollars in profits and avoid millions of dollars in trading losses. It was the first time in the seventy-five-year history of the Federal Reserve that a director was charged with fraud. Earlier, four top executives of Bevil, Bresler, a securities firm, had been convicted of fraud and given long jail terms. Their testimony during trial led to the indictment of Rough.

- In 1989, income tax evasion by Wall Streeters had become so widespread that the New York State tax department began to withhold taxes from bonuses and commissions at the state's highest rate. At least fifteen thousand Wall Street employees appeared to have filed no state income tax returns for at least one of the previous three years.

In late 1988, Drexel finally agreed to plead guilty to six counts of mail, wire, and securities fraud and to pay $650 million in fines and restitution as part of the agreement. The penalty was the largest sum ever exacted by the government for a white-collar crime. Thus ended a two-year investigation into one of Wall Street's largest and most profitable firms. The agreement would not be final until the firm settled related civil charges filed by the Securities and Exchange Commission. These charges included illegal insider trading, stock manipulation, and defrauding clients in more than a dozen deals. The $650 million was expected to be divided into a penalty paid to the government and a fund that would be used to compensate investors who claimed to be injured by conduct that Drexel admitted was illegal. But as one lawyer said, "In terms of remedying the wrongs committed, it would be folly to assume the Government even came close."

A few months later, a federal grand jury indicted Michael Milken, the Drexel executive who had transformed corporate takeovers through the pioneering use of high-yield "junk bonds." At 42, Milken had built a financial empire that brought him more than $1 billion from 1983 to 1987 and provided financing for hundreds of corporations and takeovers. He faced ninety-eight counts for cheating clients and stockholders, manipulating the marketplace, and tricking a corporation into being taken over.

In 1987 alone Milken's personal take was about $550 million. That is a pay rate of about $1.5 million a day. His wages per minute that year, day in and day out: $1,046. No one else in American history ever earned anywhere near as much in a year as Michael Milken.

That income represented the peak of a decade of greed on Wall Street, a time when the push for more money and bigger deals made the public feel that something was terribly wrong. "It's embarrassing to our financial system," said Samuel L. Hayes III, a professor of investment banking at the Harvard Business School. "It portrays the image of an industry that has gotten totally out of control in terms of its greed for money."

Of course, as we've seen, Milken was not alone. Because of deals he made possible, hundreds of millions of dollars streamed into the pockets of people on Wall Street. Hundreds of them began to make over $1 million a year. One of them said to a reporter, "A million is kind of like peanuts now."

Large fees and bonuses create big temptations. Big dollars come to equal big me. Competing frantically to be top gun, some executives may stop at nothing. Many observers of the Drexel debacle saw it not as a failure of Wall Street but of society. How, they ask, do you alter a value system that has nourished such violations of law and morality? Stephen Gillers, a law professor at New York University, commented, "We can't expect a single profession to be holier than the rest of society. To the extent that people feel that in the world at large it is OK to cut corners, they will continue to do it within their particular industry."

HOPAL PAYME
Y UNION CARBIDE
ET AT $470 MILLION

Officials'
In Bribe (

s Outline

Meese La
Received
Witness A

Wedtech Offic
Payment of $8(

BLAME IS NOT FIXED

Top Indian Court Drops
All Criminal Charges
Filed on Toxic Leak

By LEONARD BUI

ome "greedy and corru
y health inspectors simply
in the air" when they w
ants to show how large
ed from the owners —
and five fingers for $50
cutor said yesterday.
e jotted the amount th
f paper and others rul
and thumbs together
t that meant, 'I

By LYDIA CHAV

A former executive of th
Corporation testified yester
paid the personal lawyer
General Edwin Meese
$800,000 for "his in
Meese."

**Bhopal Aftermath:
4-Year Struggle**

THE ACCIDENT Methyl
isocyanate, a toxic chemical, leaked from a pesti-
...dent. Dec. 3, 1984.

3 in Sanitation
Held on Charges
nvolving Bribes

Exposing the F.D

Wedtech Executive Describes

F.D.A. has revised
ic drugs and a gra

As the "whis
strategy. The d
when Representa
Democrat who sp
gation into the
officials against
And Mylan's ac
tting a cloud
t in some

rests Relate to Payoff
Improper Dumping

By LYDIA CHAVEZ

A former executive of the Wedtech
Corporation testified yesterday that he
paid part of a $50,000 bribe to a former
Bronx Borough President by treating
him and his wife to trips to Atlantic
City and giving them as much as
$13,500 in cash for gambling and other
expenses.

The former executive, Mario Moreno, who is cooperating with the Government in exchange for leniency, testified
earlier that the former Borough President, Stanley Simon, asked for $50,000
litical and charitable
lping Wedtech push
through the New
estimate in 1984.
ed yester...

By ARNOLD H. LUBASCH

ht employees of New York
Department have be
on bribery charges in
s to remove resident
in cash

Ex-Inspector Sentenced
To Jail in Payoff Case

A retired New York City healt
spector who pleaded guilty to exto
$500 payoff from a restaurant
entenced by a Federal judge ye
ay to three months in jail and a $
ne.
In imposing the sentence in Fed
strict Court in Brooklyn, Judge
Bartels told the 59-year-old def
Joseph Sabatini, "You have
a public trust."
r. Sabatini, who now lives in Gr
Pa., was the first of 46 people
ed earlier this year on sim
ges to be sentenced. Thirty-
people, virtually all of them c
and former health inspectors a
visors, have entered guilty ple
old, about half of the City Hea
ment's former inspectors
harged with extorting hundre
sands of dollars from resta
y threatening to close them t
for sanitation violations.
w J. Maloney, the Unite
torney for the Eastern Dis
ew York, said he was satisfie
sentence imposed by Judge

key witnesses in the trial of Mr. Simon:
Representative Mario Biaggi;
Biaggi, the Congressman's son; Richard
nard G. Ehrlich, the Congressman's
former law partner, and three others.
Mr. Moreno also testified that Fred
Neuberger, another former Wedtech
executive cooperating with the Gover-
ment, suggested in 1985 that
"eliminate" John Mariotta, the com-
ny's founder and one of the defendant
because he "was a complete idiot."
Mr. Moreno said that when he
tested, Mr. Neuberger rep!
the problem with
Boy Scouts."

Ralph Lawrence, te
Mr. Moreno's
where from $7,0
the witness
expecter
cutic

Cable Execu
Says Consul
cited a
es That $2
s to Be for I

By JOSEPH P. F

le television execu
lay that a public
close to Donald
im that his comp
a Queens franchis
le to" Mr. Manes
President.
e executive, Al Sim
l-O-Vision Inc., said
hael A. Nussbaum
be money could "
per bag or an attach
a locker or Swiss ba
mon said he turned f

U.S., FOR DECADES,
LET URANIUM LEAK
AT WEAPON PLANT

RISK TO THOUSANDS

Documents Indicate a
Decision Not to Act
on Major Cleanup

Mr. Simon testified
Court in Queens in
Nussbaum, who is a
"in concert" with M
a $250,000 bribe fr
Orth-O-Vision
more," he testified
based on run
not to the pu

Bribery Inquiries Examine Newark School System

By JESUS RANGEL
Special to The New York Times

WARK, Sept. 30 — Federal and
County prosecutors are investi-
allegations that some school of-
here sold administrative jobs,
familiar with the inqu...

nas to administrators and that Essex
prosecutors had interviewed other officials.
Several administrators
high school princi...
fore a...

nacd. Mr. George did n...
The office...

☞ 11 ☜

Everybody's Doing It

WE'VE JUST LOOKED at Wall Streeters who commit white-collar crimes out of greed. Just as guilty of white-collar crime is the politician who abuses public office to put money into his or her pocket. Both are shaped by indifference to public morality and by their own lack of ethical standards. And both find vice agreeably well paid.

To start at the top of government service: more than 110 senior officials of the Reagan administration (1981–1989) came under investigation, were accused of improper conduct, resigned under fire, or had their nominations withdrawn or rejected. The former White House aide Michael Deaver is but one of the better known ones convicted of criminal conduct. In addition, several members of Congress were charged with ethical misconduct during the same years.

In the face of all this, a congressional bill to protect
federal workers who expose fraud and corruption was killed
through veto by President Ronald Reagan shortly before
he left office. The bill, unanimously adopted by both House
and Senate, would have created an independent agency to
encourage whistle-blowers and to prevent retaliation
against them.

Most Americans seem to believe that such an agency is
necessary. Recently, a national poll showed that seven out
of ten people thought illegal payoffs were common in the
federal government. Half of those polled thought the government was not honest. What else could they think when,
in addition to the frequent news reports of white-collar
crime in government, they read that as attorney general,
Edwin Meese III was accused of conflict of interest in his
ties to Wedtech, the Bronx military contractor. Again, he
was accused of conflict of interest in a project to build a
billion-dollar Iraqi oil pipeline. He resigned toward the end
of Reagan's second term after a report by an independent
prosecutor found that he had probably violated federal tax
and conflict-of-interest laws.

Examples of white-collar crime are abundant in both
state and city government. Some of the inspectors employed by the New York City Health Department simply
"put their fingers into the air" when they walked into
restaurants to show how large a payoff they wanted from
the owner. Two fingers, $200; five fingers, $500. The
scheme reached out from luxurious restaurants to small
delis and bagel shops. In some restaurants, said the federal
prosecutor, the place was "so filthy dirty" that rats scurried

about during inspection, yet the city health officials pretended they saw nothing wrong. By contrast, clean places were harassed, threatened, or closed because they did not pay a bribe. This extortion had been going on for several years when it was brought to trial; of forty-six inspectors arrested, thirty-five pleaded guilty. It was, said the prosecutor, "systematic corruption that endangered the public."

In New Jersey, some public school administrators of Essex County were alleged to have sold administrative jobs. Principals and vice-principals, it was said, had been forced to pay in order to receive promotions or jobs. This form of corruption has often been reported in many parts of the country.

Housing officials in New York were charged with accepting bribes from private contractors. Five men were arrested for steering construction and maintenance contracts to companies that would do the work on the five thousand residential buildings taken over by the city for nonpayment of taxes. In exchange for payoffs the officials approved substandard work and inflated bills submitted by the contractors. The accused men each earned about $30,000 a year and had taken about $15,000 in bribes. Some of them spent the money gambling at Atlantic City casinos.

In the previously mentioned Wedtech case, a $50,000 bribe was paid to the Bronx borough president for helping the military contractor push a real estate deal through the New York City Board of Estimate. Part of the bribe consisted of free trips to Atlantic City and thousands in cash for gambling and other expenses. Wedtech executives were charged with turning the company into a racketeering enterprise that paid millions of dollars to get government contracts. One of its executives testified that he paid the personal lawyer of Edwin Meese about $800,000 for "his influence on Ed Meese," and $80,000 to Bronx Congressman Robert Garcia in return for "political favors and political introductions." Garcia was convicted of taking bribes.

Corruption even infects organizations set up to avoid criminal behavior. Agencies called public authorities were established originally "to put public enterprises on their own feet and on their own responsibility, to free them from political interference, bureaucracy and red tape, while at the same time retaining adequate controls." Those were the words of Austin J. Tobin, longtime director of the Port Authority of New York and New Jersey.

But many public authorities have failed to develop adequate protections against abuse, judging by the lengthening list of corruption cases. The facts are not easy to come by, for the national crime surveys do not list such cases as a separate category. But Diana B. Henriques in her exhaustive study, *The Machinery of Greed: Public Authority Abuse and What to Do About It,* has found ample evidence. She has written that sometimes it has been a public authority official who was the abuser, through kickback schemes or embezzlement or political favoritism. In other cases, outsiders have taken advantage of poor agency controls to ignore the agency's public obligations.

For example, imagine an authority engineer about to

make a decision: What route should a sewer line take? The decision will increase or diminish the value of the land involved. Which contractor should be selected for the sewer line? The company chosen will make a profit and the union doing the work will have jobs for their members and dues for their treasury. If the authority engineer is free to make such decisions that can affect the pocketbook, the opening for corruption is there.

In her book Henriques pinpointed the factors that may lead officials into this kind of white-collar crime. They are "low visibility, complexity, confusing or inadequate management controls, and an absence of clear accountability."

Consider an official tempted to commit such a crime. The official tells himself or herself, "Hey, nobody's watching! Even if someone is watching, who could figure it out? If they did figure it out, they still wouldn't be able to find any evidence of it in this mess. And even if they find something, they'll never be able to pin it on me. . . ."

Once such an official begins to think this way, he or she is likely to take the step over the line toward criminal behavior.

Where codes of behavior are weak or vague or ambiguous some people have a hard time making the moral choice to avoid a criminal act. Or perhaps their agency gives them mixed signals. A top executive agency may praise socially responsible behavior in general but, when it comes to promotions, pick the staff member who saves money by cutting costs at the public's expense. Take a police department as another example. The chief may praise officers who respect the citizens' civil rights but promote the cops who make the most arrests, even when they use illegal "rough 'em up" methods.

Then there is peer pressure and the harm it can do to ethical behavior. If "everybody's doing it" and what's being done is illegal or immoral, it's hard for the lone individual to resist. For one thing, he or she may ask, if all the other people in the outfit are doing it, can it really be that bad? Moreover, when just about everybody's involved, how can the boss punish them all?

If someone chooses not to go along with a corrupt system, the risk is ostracism—being shut out by all the others—or even worse.

The decisions made nowadays by public authorities involve huge sums of money. These agencies build mass transit systems and public power plants. They renew city waterfronts and develop whole neighborhoods and towns. They construct new convention centers and sports complexes. They build airports and sewer plants and race tracks and zoos and museums and port facilities and highways and nuclear generators. They spend far beyond the average person's imagination. Hundreds of millions, even billions of dollars.

Temptation? To offer but one example of how corrupt a public agency can become, look at the Rhode Island Housing and Mortgage Finance Corporation (RIHMFC). Reporters at the Providence *Journal-Bulletin* uncovered a pattern of corruption at RIHMFC in the early 1980s. Years later, an investigation by the state attorney general led to charges against the agency's executive director, Ralph A. Pari. He was accused of embezzlement, obstruction of justice, illegally destroying agency computer records, and engaging in "racketeering activities" that had gone on for a long time. Under Pari's twelve-year tenure, according to the findings of the agency, RIHMFC had favored "friends" with mortgages at very low interest rates while refusing those rates to the general public. It had neglected poor neighborhoods while financing luxury condos in rich neighborhoods. Pari himself, at the agency's expense, had been living the high life: elegant cars, private clubs, five-star hotels and restaurants.

It was one more proof of how greed can lead to abuse of power. Dr. Annmarie Walsh, a student of public authority government, has said, "Public authorities tend to reflect the politics of the area. If those politics are corrupt, then the public authority can become the ideal vehicle for carrying out political or special interest. The more 'autonomous' they are, the more ideal they are."

'Crack House' Fire: Justice or Vi~

By ISABEL WILKERSON
Special to The New York Times

DETROIT — The working-
families on Barlow Street
sed to hurr ~ children
oors and h
nenever the
e nearby c
Two of the
e drug t
ey set i
oudly a
rly in
rry K
gelo P
ty of
mati
2-rid
bou

The Drug Bill's $2.3 Billion Promis

It was a moving sight: 12,000 police officers,
 the force, massed in Saturday's cold to
~gues slain on a single evening last
ence added weight to Police Com-
s defiant challenge to drug murder-
ill never give up. The police officers
never give up."
nination alone isn't enough; the drug
uires support from Washington. On'
the funeral, the Senate acted o
gislation, but left the dirty "
ey to the next Congress
w law began in th
ellicose posturi
gally seize
eral d

Still, one aspect of the bill deser
dramatically expands the Federal co
drug treatment. The need is obvious.
tire of slavery to drugs, yet those who
likely to be told they must wait weeks
then mo~ on may have faded.
mak~ nt on request an expl
eral funds for drug
s to reduce waiting
nt, it sharply sh
the drug budge
tion, as oppose
rdiction. The
otes more th
ction.

Military Role In Drug War
Restrained Goals Set by Conferees on Bill

By SUSAN RASKY
Special to The New York Times

WASHINGTON, June 23 — The
on clamor in Congress last month to enlis~
ill the military in the war on drugs
he given way to a more sober asses
r of what the armed forces can a
not do to halt the flow of drugs
the nation's borders.

News Analysis

The legislative result
contained in a compro-
mise $299 billion military
program bill that carves at
out a much narrower role
r the military in the drug effort than
ommended by either the House or
Senate. Although House and Senate
tiators are still working out other
details of the bill, provisions deal-
ith military involvement in drug
ction have been settled.
se provisions scrap measures
by the House and Senate that,
other things, would have per-
military personnel to make
rests, a prospect that had set
bells at the Pentagon and
vil liberties groups. i-
romise stipul-
ces con
onitorin
hat Pen
much n.
y milita
compr
eyond t
recomm
nti-drug
at the n
ompron
time es
mal mi

Poll Finds 90% Favor Keeping Drugs Illicit

By The Associated Press

Nine of 10 Americans reject decrimi-
nalizing all illicit drugs, with a majority saying legalization would lead to
increased drug use, according to an
W.   ABC News poll.
new mo
lion is a   In addition, 70 percent of those polled
must com   said they wanted the Federal Govern-
try at Yale   ment to increase spending to prevent
rien of drug a   drug abuse.
ing here in ma   The legalization of marijuana was
consensus has   favored by 25 percent of those polled,
that this drug pr   but only 7 percent favo~ the legaliza-
On April 25, Ma   tion of cocaine and 6 ~ .he her-
of Baltimore shock   oin should be legal.
ates Conference of   The nationwide t
.Schmoke   adults conducted fr
a meeting of the   ~ole."
legal drug consumption should

Sept. 1 showed that 51 percent of those
surveyed said they believed legalizing
drugs would lead to increased drug use.
Eleven percent said use would decrease and 38 percent said it would
make no difference.

The margin of sampling error for the
poll, released Tuesday, was plus or
minus 5 percentage points.

Asked whether all illicit drugs should
be legalized, 9 percent said they should
be and 90 percent said they should not.

By a margin of 2 to 1, 47 percent to 23
percent, those polled said the legaliza-
~ of drugs would lead to an increase

ange. Atte
ely ackno
atments
known
should
23 less
edu
ea
estme
ndsome p
d crime. But s
speculative M

Fearful and Angry Flo
Erect Street Barriers

By JEFFREY SCHMALZ
Special to The New York Times

MIAMI, Dec. 5 — After leveling off in
the middle part of the decade, crime is
rising sharply in parts of the Miami-
Fort Lauderdale area, and some residents are so fearful and so fed up that
they are barricading their neighborhood streets to keep criminals out.

In many areas, just one short residential block or cul de sac is blocked to
cars and, therefore, to criminals cruis-
ing for easy pickings. But in a dozen
areas, whole neighborhoods are
blocked off by bright orange barrels,
forcing cars onto main arteries.

Although the roads are public, some
of the dozen neighborhoods also have
or plan checkpoints where private
guards lower gates to stop cars, question drivers and write down license
numbers.
the barricades are being
a vote by a neigh-
proval b

the streets o
selected few.

The lawyer
houses are
technically,
cars to pas
them. Priva
u.nat cost
related crim
and the to
than $33 bi
ductivity t
are fered by he
Alcohol,
used by a
The study
costs soci
$2.6 billic
costs,
came fr
motor v
deaths ar
rrhosis
Federa
but 18
then least
aine

Rescuing The Drug Bill

U nder the pressures of an election year and of a public in
near-hysteria over the drug
problem, Congress has been debating
some horrendously punitive, in many
cases irrelevant "remedies." But as
its last official act, the 100th Congress
passed an anti-drug bill that critics —
including me — are bound to concede
is much less offensive than expected.

By far the greatest significance of
the new bill is in its drastic shift of
funds from law enforcement and interdiction — neither of which has
been able to stop or slow the drug epidemic — to preventive and treatment
programs. In fiscal 1989, newly available funds will be divided fifty-fifty
between these overall functions, although President Reagan had proposed that 72 percent go to enforcement and interdiction. In fiscal 1990,
55 percent will go to treatment and
prevention grants and programs.

Part of the political price of that
important change in direction was
authorization of the death penalty —
a provision that deludes its hopeful,
and shames its cynical, supporters.

Schmoke, a former prosecu-
he had been sickened by the
law-enforcement officials at
of drug traffickers.
ed support for hearings from
nald M. Fraser of Minneap-
Fortney H. (Pete)
at who is

galizing Drugs – Step

nty Hospital has the feel
nt. The battered bodies
eams that pass through
night are constant re-
e have lost the conven-
st drugs.
course, are not the
end up in the emer-
ug-related violence
he point where inno-
hot every week, and
ug dealers and as-
killed at a rate of

such proposals ring hollow. Obviously, the lure of making fast nontaxable
money through the illegal drug trade
far outweighs the risk not only of
prison but of death.

I realize that no one gets elected to
public office by taking the wrong side

Look at the
By removing
would substa
lence that goe
and the stree
drug habits. It
of police offic
standers caugh
would allow be
the chance of d
transmission of
dles.
The beneficial
ties

Solutions to other ills
will follow

By K

n Decen
the dea
year-old
younger
his moth
pain. This
y for a
rk City's
bush sectio
nths later,
n as I pron

RROW'S

he Next N

ths come early to
d have been lead-
stead of pursuing
which

☞ 12 ☜

Unless You Take Action, We Will

WHAT CAN society do to protect itself against crime and criminals? Let's examine first the dangerous drugs and the crimes committed because of them.

In today's United States the people look to their government to guard them against the powerful threat of illegal drugs. On every level—federal, state, local—agencies responsible for research, education, enforcement, care, and cure are pressed to increase their efforts. Research tells us the facts about drugs—which are harmful, and in what ways. But much of the public has yet to agree on what to do to halt the drug epidemic. The campaign against addiction needs to begin with the young. Schools are starting to teach courses about the danger of drugs from the earliest years. Today it is just as important to know about heroin and crack and speed and what they can do to the human body and spirit as it is to know the causes of the American Revolution. Not only the school, but parents, churches, clubs, youth groups, and the mass media need to present the hard evidence.

As with all crime, law-enforcement agencies come into play when prevention fails. Ramsey Clark has pointed out:

No area of police activity calls for greater skill or discipline than drug control. Of all consensual crimes, the victim here is least reliable and least likely to cooperate. His dependence on his supplier is great. Most traffickers are users themselves and therefore doubly dangerous—dangerous as persons dealing in serious crime and dangerous as unstable individuals under the influence of narcotics.

In 1974, recognizing the immense danger, Congress established the U.S. Drug Enforcement Administration. It is the primary but not the only U.S. agency involved in drug enforcement. In recent years, more than a dozen House and Senate committees and subcommittees have taken some responsibility on drug-related issues. In the course of their investigations, different positions on the drug issue have been taken. The most widely supported view is that the government needs harsher drug laws, stricter enforcement, and more severe penalties for those who break those laws. According to this viewpoint, the military should do more to halt drugs from coming across our borders and foreign governments should be strongly pressured to stop the production of drugs for export. More funding for education and rehabilitation programs is desired, too.

A small group of legislators argue that banning drugs is a self-defeating policy. The constitutional amendment prohibiting alcohol in the 1920s and early 1930s didn't work. Those against banning drugs believe it's better not to try to prevent all drug use by all people at all costs but, instead, to take drug distribution away from the criminals. Control and regulate it carefully, they say, and treat drug abusers as a public health problem. They point to smoking tobacco and drinking alcoholic beverages as examples of how strong habits *can* be changed. Americans do less of both today, they argue, not because the army jails tobacco growers in North Carolina or bombs whiskey stills in Scotland, but because attitudes change with the help of strong education and treatment programs.

Still a third group in Congress believes it foolish and wasteful to spend countless billions building new prisons, spraying herbicides on South American jungles, and x-raying tourists returning from vacation. But they don't advocate making the use of dangerous drugs legal. Rather, they call for a measured battle against both drug supply and demand, while waiting for the drug epidemic to fall off on its own. They claim that few people any longer abuse LSD, mescaline, or opium, drugs that were popular not so long ago.

Out of a mixture of these views came the omnibus drug bill Congress adopted late in 1988. It called for a $6.1 billion budget. Rather than putting most of the emphasis on law enforcement and halting drug imports at the border, it assigned the greater part of the drug budget to treatment and education. It was a wise change. Attempts to cut the flow of drugs into the country have failed, while some drug treatments are known to be successful. The law provides money for research to find a drug that could block the craving for cocaine, much as methadone blocks the craving for heroin.

A much debated feature of the new law is a death penalty. It is limited to murders occurring as part of major drug offenses and to killers of police officers during drug-related crimes. The question of the death penalty flares up in almost every election campaign. Opponents of the death penalty ask: Has the fear of the death penalty deterred an addict who shoots a candy-store owner for a few dollars? Will the death penalty stop drug dealers from chasing after vast profits from their trade? Drug dealers know that death is their occupational hazard. It may come from another dealer's gun, from an overdose, from contaminated drugs, from the dirty needle that bring AIDS. When drug dealers are murdered every day, the death penalty is an empty threat. It takes attention away from more important anti-drug measures.

Only a small part of the total drug budget was made available by the Congress in 1988. The rest is supposed to come from cuts in other parts of the budget or from new taxes. It remains to be seen whether the Bush administration and the Congress will follow through on the promise made in 1988.

With government moving so slowly into action, the frustrated people of the drug-ridden inner cities sometimes take justice into their own hands. In Detroit two neighbors got tired of the drug trading and turf wars and set a nearby crack house on fire. They proudly admitted it in court, and the jury acquitted them of arson. In Manhattan, citizens staged undercover drug buys and made citizen's arrests of drug dealers. On Long Island, a man fired his shotgun at a crowd he believed to be dealing in drugs and wounded a woman nearby. In Miami, angry residents burned down thirty-five crack houses in two weeks. In East Harlem, a man known to be a drug addict was attacked and killed by a crowd after he robbed a woman of twenty dollars.

Citizens were saying to the authorities, "Unless you take action, we will." An official of the Federal Drug Enforcement Agency said he saw "the surge of community activism on drugs as both a sign of hope and of danger. Communities can play a critical role in fighting the drug trade. But if people begin to lose faith in the criminal justice system," he warned, they will begin to act like a lynch mob.

Around the country thousands of community groups were staging protests, organizing street patrols, and trying any tactic possible to regain control of their blocks and buildings. The Citizens Committee for New York has helped train hundreds of neighborhood groups in antidrug tactics. "The vast number of urban dwellers," said Felice Jergens, a committee organizer, "are dissatisfied with Mrs. Reagan's 'Just Say No.' " She added that it's wrong to blame the individual's lack of discipline for the massive social problem of addiction.

One group on Manhattan's West Side taught hundreds of residents how to identify the "runners," the "steerers," and the drug hiding places of crack dealers. They coordinated merchant watches to help the police clear out some of their neighborhood's worst crack-dealing hangouts.

In New York, the police have trained dozens of community groups to conduct neighborhood patrols. The patrollers are encouraged to observe drug dealing and pass information anonymously to the police. They are instructed not to take action against dealers themselves. So angry have some people become that they set up tenant guards in their buildings who warn drug buyers that if they enter they might not come out alive. Yes, it's risky to confront addicts, one man said, but is it any more risky than to let them take over your building and your street?

Some big cities are bringing police officers into the classroom to help keep young people off drugs and away from crime. The officers teach pupils about the dangers of drugs and how to shield themselves from the pressures of peers and pushers. At the same time, teachers are educated to recognize early signs of drug abuse.

We've looked at some of the steps being taken to combat the drug epidemic. But however important, it is only one aspect of crime. To get a complete picture of crime in the United States it's necessary to look at the system of justice itself. How was it created? And how well does it work?

How Technology Is Arming Today's Law Enforce

Drugs Seen as an Increasing Threat to Poli

Valerie Block

"... you did the whole
... ecialist," com-
... worked in
... de-

By TODD S. PURDUM

... en years after the Knapp Commis-
... nd pervasive corruption in the New
... Police Department, criminal-jus-
... ts and police commanders warn
... nt drug trafficking and efforts to
... re posing extraordinary ...
... ats to the integrity of the force.
... onths, six officers or former
... been chair
... the Bronx
... or robb
... a drug
... ected

of gun was used with a bullet, which bears
the signature markings of the lands—raised
surfaces—and grooves of the gun. "This is
as good as fingerprints," said Mr. Quirk,
who noted that if a criminal tried to file
down a barrel of a gun to erase the mark-
... he might erase the lands but the
... ould remain to identify the gun.
... d that cartridge shells can
... t, as they, too, are
... when the gun
... claims a
... that

trajectories, Mr. Quirk said
that they are judged to be too
the Police Department.

Mr. Quirk testified for the
that there was no way, give
their bullet wounds, that M
tims could have been sitting
car where they were shot
played a large role in his te
half of the police officer
Bumpurs. Of the four woun
elderly woman, who wa
apartment from which the
seeking to have her evicted
... d that two apparently
... fire and sugges
... Ms. Bump
... ties

circumstances made it necessary for police
departments to be more vigilant than ever.
Criminologists generally agree that
sweeping policy changes since 1972 have
done much to control, or even eradicate,
some kinds of corruption, like systematic
payoffs from gambling operators, a practice that the Knapp investigation found was
common and was tolerated.

New Drug Unit
Checks Police
On Corruption

n Officer Is Arrested
Undercover Squad

By DAVID E. PITT

w York City Police Departme
eep narcotics corruption fro
mong officers, has establi
cover squad to look f
at the precinct level
er squad, called
... and prevent
... hs ago, par
... s broug
... rug e
... p

Officers have been
charged with robbing
dealers at gunpoint.

... Temptation
... re is especially vul-
... w because of the re-
... re than 17,000 offi-
... which drug use is
... same time, an explo-
... as prompted Police
... in Ward to use uni-
... considered among
... corruption, to try to
... e o
... people wor
... lot of inform
... care who
... at wh

stem the trade in drugs.
"Today you have a generation of
officers who grew up where dr
common," said Thomas A
dent of the Citizen
New York C
neigh

Fugitives Vanish E
Overworked Police

nals to the Punch

... e police
... w try
... to deal with
... problems
... that spawn
... crime.

grant public drug use.
In his first effort, Operation Pres-
sure Point, on the Lower East Side, with officers
the streets were flooded with dealers and
who arrested low-level customers.
frightened away customers.
Pressure Point's successor is the
Community Patrol Officer Program,
in which 750 officers are assigned to
neighborhood beats in 75 precincts.
However, gang warfare in some
city neighborhoods is so bad that
community-oriented policing may
have to take a back seat to the need of
getting terrorists off the street. So
far, no textbook strategy for wresting
control of a neighborhood from a
street gang has yet been found.
To solve community problems, the
... have to solve their own, as
... int illustrated. Driving
... streets can ex

By SELWYN RAAB

In many ways, Clovis Fearon
atched the profile of New York
y's typical criminal fugitive.
e was wanted on a drug-related
e, had few roots in the com-
and to escape detection
'o a new address and assumed
me, Anthony Dixon.
s like Mr. Fearon who are
for violent or well-publi-
and who make an effort
ppear into the city are
ble to catch, the police
number of fugitives
officers specifi-
them

of crimes. The num
rants issued for
creased 31 percent
years to 154,721
118,324 in 1982, the
ment said.

Much of the incre
by criminal justice e
in drug use in the ci
use of crack, the p
form of cocaine.
ures were rising slo
80's but they so
arrival o

Fighting Crime Wholesale and Retail

What's the best way to prosecute crime? The
a standard answer is, one case at a time. Yet the
limits of that approach have long been clear, and
some criminal justice authorities are pondering a
broader strategy that helps fight crime wholesale
rather than retail. The concept is by now familiar to
There may be an even stronger case for it
... among district attorneys.
In the early 1980's, some police departments
an experimenting with "problem-oriented" policing. Instead of simply responding to burglaries
that occur near a vacant lot where addic... congre-
for example, the police might organize neigh-
... up the lot, keep an eye on it and push
... to bring in more drug treatment.
... wn results. In a paper
... rvard, Ron-

executive agencies. Standing between the po
the courts, they are well positioned to analy
lems and devise a coordinated response.
In Brooklyn, District Attorney Elizab
man has claimed success for a progra
quires turnstile jumpers and other transi
to clean subway stations. Janet Reno,
ney for Dade County, Florida, shows
concept might be extended.
In 1985, she persuaded the county a
system to support one of her prosecu
Tom Petersen, who tried fighting cri
in the city's housing projects. He me
to sponsor day care, health and
grams and helped the service-
dwellers set up their own succes
stores.

Prosecutors need to be ready
ividual case. But the arithme
In New York City, an

☞ 13 ☜

The Enforcers

POLICE AND PRISONS, judges and juries, trials, lawyers, legislators—these are familiar to us all. They're part of the American system of law, part of our common culture.

It is impossible to present a picture of crime in the United States without looking into law enforcement and the administration of justice. When a crime is committed, the police step in to find the offender. Then the courts take over for indictment, trial, and, should the accused be convicted, sentencing. If the sentence calls for jailing, the prisons are next.

This is all woven into the system of criminal justice under which we live. From the beginning of our nation, local government has been the seat of law enforcement. Sheriffs and the police are the officers of the law. Above that base are county, state, and federal officers. By the late

1980s the public safety industry in this country included more than 17,000 police departments, employed more than 400,000 people, imprisoned more than a half million convicts, and cost $28 billion a year.

Local law enforcement covers more than 40,000 jurisdictions. The citizens of any locality rely on their police officers to keep them safe, to protect them against crime. For law enforcement to be effective, it must be close to the people it serves. It must be aware of their needs and problems, it must be able to sense community changes, and it must anticipate the measures change requires.

With crime so overwhelming a problem, some advocate the replacement of local police by a national police force. They claim greater professionalization and better officering would be the result. But the diversity of a country so vast as the United States argues against that. Each village, each city, has its own history, habits, ethnic and racial makeup, economic levels, mobility, and many other factors that cast doubt on the value of a uniform approach to crime.

Another argument against a national police force is the immense power it would concentrate in one person's hands. Anyone familiar with the terrors of a Gestapo in Hitler's Germany or a KGB in the Soviet Union knows there is reason to shy away from a federal police force. As it is, the technological developments in police work continually increase the ability of the government to keep its eye on the individual citizen. Advances in computers and electronic communications make it possible to penetrate into everyone's life until none of us can any longer live a completely anonymous existence.

Beyond highway patrol, states do not employ a large number of police. The federal government plays a much bigger part in law enforcement. In many of its agencies, officers enforce customs law, tax collection, and agricultural, postal, and drug inspection. The federal government also reinforces local police where crimes cross state lines, for example in interstate theft and kidnapping. The federal agencies such as the FBI offer research, financial resources, and leadership in crime detection to all parts of the country.

The way local policing has developed in the United States makes high quality and effectiveness almost impossible, say the experts. On the average, police districts have ten officers, but many have only one. How can one or a few protect a community twenty-four hours a day, seven days a week, all the year round? A single large county may have scores of separate police districts within its borders. A drunken or drugged driver or a fleeing bandit tearing down the highway passes through several police jurisdictions in no time. A criminal plotting to start some illegal operation in such a crazy-quilt pattern of policing has his or her pick of which jurisdiction is most likely to be corruptible. While a national police force may be undesirable, perhaps there should be fewer local police departments, and those organized on a more rational basis.

A serious handicap for the police is society's habit of dumping unenforceable laws on them. Legislatures find it easy to pass laws they know will not be respected by the public. Such laws muster the police against drunkenness, gambling, prostitution, and other offenses that experience

shows will never be stopped by force. A significant amount
of police time goes into such cases because of our hypocrisy
in refusing to face the truth about human behavior.

Law enforcement was once a fairly simple task. But the
police department today, in a city of any size, needs to
include on its staff experts in chemistry, physics, elec-
tronics, computers, medicine, psychology, social work,
human relations, race relations, marriage, and youth
counseling. Ideally, each officer should command at least
some of these capacities, and perform them well.

The community relies on the police for safety, for the
protection of life and property, for justice. But the rights
of the individual guaranteed in the U.S. Constitution mean
little if the police do not respect them. The *Miranda* decision, for example, requires police at the time of arrest
to warn suspects that they need not make a statement;
that if they do, it can be used against them; that they are
entitled to a lawyer; and that one will be provided if re-
quested. Supreme Court decisions bearing on this and
other rights exist only on paper unless the police carry
them out.

The education of police officers is all-important. If they
are to do their job well, they must understand what it is
they are trying to do. "This requires," Ramsey Clark has
written,

an understanding of the dynamics of our people. They [the
police] deal with every aspect of society and often at times of
highest emotionalism. Officers, black and white, policing a black
ghetto must be thoroughly familiar with life in the ghetto—its

patterns, its habits and needs, its personalities and powers. Somehow police must understand the motivations of youths who commit most crime and the family disorders that start children toward lives of crime. Anything less than sensitive understanding is dangerous—dangerous for the police, dangerous for society.

What is the law the police are called upon to enforce? Where did it come from?

Large firms beef up criminal defense

By PHYLLIS FURMAN
CRAIN'S NEW YORK BUSINESS

g white coll

Just two months ago, Charles Carberry was earning a living making the likes of Dennis Levine and Ivan Boesky sleep. As chief of the Securities and Commodities Fraud Unit of the U.S. ...ey's office, the 38-year-... ...rheaded the biggest ...stigation in leg... ...t Mr. Car...

...lars Spurring a Rethinking

eminist 'Wide Diversity Seen on Spending to Defend

By TAMAR LEW!

WASHINGTON, Sept. 5 (AP) — The 50 states and the District of Columbia spend widely differing amounts to represent criminal defendants who cannot afford a lawyer, the Justice Department reported today.

s more women have ool professors, they efine legal theory t y see as the distin es of women.

In a flood of recer nals, feminis ng a basic the do it that year.

The department said that, in 1986, Arkansas spent the least for indigent defendants — an average of 69 cents per state resident. The District of Columbia spent the most, $29 per capita, that year.

...was compiled by the Bu an update

The average per capita expenditure nationwide was $4.11 in 1986, up from $2.76 in 1982. There were about 4.5 million cases in 1986 in which a public defender was appointed, up about 40 percent in the four-year period.

When average costs per indigent case were computed, Arkansas again was last, spending $63 per case in 1986. New Jersey was first, spending an average of $540.

Landmark Case Is Recalled

Nationwide, the average cost per case was $223 in 1986, up from $196 in

...report said.

v. Wainright in 1963, when the ...tended the right to counsel courts to all indigent defe charged with a felony.

Some states have expanded th gram to include representation fo ceedings involving parole, proba parental rights, civil commitment post-conviction matters.

Fireworks

GR...

Trust the people and

Turner

HY is it that argu- ...ents about reform- ...e our ramshackle ...overnment so often ...question whether ...s charter of fun ...oms to pre ...ges of t ...her issue ...House ...n seem ...iting, the ...al politi...

Confident State, like Britain or America today, is general- liberal democracy ... different political v... treats its citizens... and respect ... like those ... time

U.S. Sets Up Task Forces on Market Fraud

By KURT EICHENWALD

Special to The New York Times

WASHINGTON, Jan. 31 — The Justice Department will establish task forces in six cities in coordination with other Federal agencies to combat fraud in the nation's securities and commodities markets, Attorney General Dick Thornburgh said today.

The plan for a permanent, broad structure for fighting financial fraud follows almost ...gations of the ...have rocked

cently disclosed undercover investigation of possible fraud on the nation's two largest commodities exchanges, in Chicago.

The plan is the first attempt by top Justice Department officials to make the prosecution of such cases a permanent priority.

Until now, Government investigations of securities and commodities fraud cases have been developed in response to particular situations, with teams of investigators assembled by United States Attorneys. The proposal was first submitted in ...1987 by Rudolph W.

Giuliani, the United States Attorney in Manhattan, who has led the Government's assault on Wall Street corruption. But Attorney General Edwin Meese 3d did not act on it.

Mr. Thornburgh said the task forces were needed because white-collar crime against investors was more pervasive than officials had thought five years ago.

"The problem is bad enough that we want to take some extra steps to

Continued on Page D5

Shoddy Lawyers Called Court T

By WILLIAM GLABERSON

Lawyers in New York City courts are increasingly concealing facts, baiting judges and using other tactics that obscure the truth, judges and legal experts told a hearing panel yesterday.

A subcommittee of the City Bar As...

egal Services: Answering the Call

Two years ago, an Iowa attorney named John ...llard was asked by a Federal court to defend ...gent inmates who had accused prison officials ...istreatment. His answer was a surprising "no." ...Mallard said he might volunteer for a securities ...ankruptcy case, but he wasn't a civil rights liti-... The court ordered him to take the case any-... Mr. Mallard sued, took his own case to the ...ed States Supreme Court — and won, 5 to 4. ...e Court was plainly correct to rule that the ...ry-old Federal statute authorizing judges to

fortable livelihoods to a legal system that frequently requires their unpaid help. Indeed, the need is so great that many top judges and bar leaders now call for mandatory givebacks in the form of donated service. And there was nothing in the Court's ruling that would prevent Congress or the states from giving judges the power to conscript lawyers under more clearly worded authority.

But even mandatory programs won't meet the mounting need. The Federal Legal Services Corporation which th...

☞ 14 ☜

Justice:
Imperfect but
Improvable

THE LAW as we know it now wasn't always this way. Like any living system, it grew and developed as the times changed. Some of the law is very ancient; some made only yesterday. It is built layer upon layer, the old modified by the new, but not always disappearing. It's a gradual, piecemeal process, with few really radical changes.

American law is different from other systems of justice because it *is* American and is rooted in our history. Every society has laws to govern itself and settle disputes. The systems of law work with varying degree of effectiveness. But whatever the results, the law, as Lawrence M. Friedman, professor of law at Stanford University, has said, "does the bidding of those whose hands are on the controls. The law of China, the United States, Nazi Germany, and . . . South Africa reflect the goals and policies of those who call the tune in those societies."

No matter what the historical background, what's important about law is how it works in the here and now. The passions of today, the economic pressures, the political drives, are central to understanding the functioning of the law.

The Europeans who came here when this continent belonged to the Native Americans were of many different ethnic and cultural groups. They came in force and left their traces on the law. But during the long colonial era the English prevailed and the English common law became the dominant system. Transplanted to American shores, that system underwent many changes to adapt to conditions in the New World.

In the United States there are fifty-two separate legal systems—those of the states plus the District of Columbia and the federal court system. There are ninety-five federal district courts, twelve circuit courts of appeal, and the Supreme Court.

The system as a whole is based upon the common law. It is different from most European systems of law. Theirs is a modernized version of Roman law expressed in codes. Their judges are bound by the specific provisions of a code and not by previous judicial interpretations and precedents that have built up over the centuries.

The common law, on the other hand, is expressed in the rulings judges make when they decide cases. Legislatures make laws, of course, but the ultimate, the highest source of law is found in the decisions of judges. Common law, as Friedman has put it, is "judge-made law, molded, refined, examined, and changed in the crucible of actual decision, and handed down from generation to generation in the form of reported cases."

Precedent—what other judges had decided earlier—became the general rule of common law. In theory, people used to believe that the common law was not human-made. Somehow the judges "found" the law or uncovered it. But in modern times the law is seen as made by people, as a tool to achieve certain ends. Law is not a divine creation or a fixed body of rules that tells people where they belong in the order of society and what they can do or not do. It's an instrument that the people at the levers of power use to move toward some particular goal. The law changes constantly as human needs and desires change.

Operating under these general principles or rules are two major classes of law, the civil and the criminal. Civil law spells out the rights and duties that exist between citizens and their governments. If you infringe on the legally recognized rights of another, civil law is involved. For example, if a mechanic repairs your car and fails to put back an important part and you are then injured while driving, you can sue for damages. You bring a civil action in court. You're the plaintiff or the person suing and the mechanic or garage owner is the defendant or the person being sued.

Criminal law deals with a wrong committed against the public as a whole. Criminal acts are defined by local or state governments or by the federal government through laws passed by legislative bodies. In a criminal case the government seeks to impose a penalty upon a person found guilty. In a civil case, one party tries to make the other party carry out a duty or pay for the damages caused by the failure to do so. In the case of an alleged crime the accused is prosecuted by a public official, who represents society as a whole.

A word about the classes of crime: They are felonies or misdemeanors, according to their seriousness. A felony is more serious and is punishable by jailing in a federal or state prison for more than a year, or by death. A misdemeanor is punished by a fine or by confinement for less than one year.

Let's look at lawyers before we discuss how they operate in the courts.

Lawyers are found everywhere in American life, in village and city, in the legislature, in the governor's mansion, in the White House, in the courts, and in the corporations. Some citizens complain of an overabundance: the United States has 267 lawyers per thousand people while Japan, an equally advanced nation, has only 0.10 lawyers per thousand people. Two out of every three lawyers on this planet live in the United States, yet we are only one-sixth of the world's population. Washington, D.C., our national capital, boasts having one lawyer for every sixty persons.

In the United States today, there are 675,000 lawyers. An additional 40,000 are turned out by the law schools every year. If this rate of increase keeps up, there will be more than a million lawyers before the year 2000. It is a profession that has never been popular. Almost four hundred years ago, Shakespeare had a character in his play *Henry VI* exclaim, "The first thing we do, let's kill all the lawyers." And wise old Ben Franklin had Poor Richard say,

"God works wonders now and then. Behold! a lawyer, an honest man!"

In 1988, a survey by the California Bar Association showed that three of every four people had a poor opinion of lawyers, and from direct dealings with them. The study concluded that lawyers are seen "as arrogant people who create problems, not solve them, and who are not concerned about their clients or about the public at large." The lawyers themselves thought their colleagues self-seeking (45 percent) or overbearing (59 percent). It was the Watergate scandal that sank the profession to a new low in the public eye. Richard Nixon, the president who had to flee the White House to escape impeachment, was a lawyer, and he was surrounded by lawyers who "made their names symbols of contempt for the law," wrote a *New York Times* columnist. But one needs to remember that it was lawyers, as prosecutors and judges, who brought their colleagues to justice. Weren't Jefferson and Madison and Adams and Lincoln lawyers, too?

For a long time lawyers have been a powerful force in the national life. They make deals and break them. They write the laws and provide the loopholes. Throughout our history they have gained more and more influence as policymakers for industrial, financial, and political interests.

While there are lawyers aplenty for the great corporations, there are far fewer for the weak and the poor. The profession affirms its duty to make legal services available without regard to the client's ability to pay. In the 1960s, the Office of Economic Opportunity (OEO) established a Legal Services Program, financed by the taxpayers, to serve that purpose. Outside that framework there are a number of private lawyers who do *pro bono* work.

How are cases tried in the American courts of law? The concept that governs trials is called the adversary system. It is a system that is staunchly upheld by most professionals connected with the law and criticized by a minority who find it unfair.

First, what is the adversary system? It is simply a system of rules of procedure. The rules are meant to keep the judge from taking sides. He or she must hold back on judgment until all the evidence has been examined and all the arguments have been heard. Neither judge nor jury is supposed to take sides on the proceedings. A fair trial requires that each side of the controversy be thoroughly presented. This is where the advocate, the lawyer for the defense, comes in. The advocate's job is to persuade the jury of the rightness of his or her case. The advocate is not expected to be detached, but to present the case in a way that will be most favorable to his or her client. The system expects the accused to be defended by a skilled lawyer, pledged to protect the rights of the accused and to present proofs and reasoned arguments on behalf of the accused. If the accused cannot afford to pay for a lawyer, the court appoints a lawyer to represent him or her.

It is perfectly proper for a lawyer to take on a criminal case and defend a person whom he or she believes to be guilty. The ethical standards of the legal profession endorse that. The lawyer is not obliged to defend a guilty person. It's up to the lawyer to decide whether he or she wishes to defend a person, no matter how guilty or innocent the accused appears to be. Even lawyers who firmly believe a client is guilty may find some unexpected turn in the evidence that proves the client is innocent. At any rate, what is important under the system is that those accused be defended by lawyers pledged to see that their rights are protected. Lawyers, so the argument goes, are not present in court merely to represent their clients. They also represent society's vital interest in the fundamental process of social decision. Of course, by the rules lawyers are not supposed to cast suspicion on innocent persons in order to free their clients.

The prosecutor is the other half of the adversary system. The prosecutor, too, does his or her best to present proofs and arguments to convince the jury that the accused is guilty of whatever crime he or she was brought to trial for.

The adversary procedure is like combat. Its focus is on determining guilt or innocence. It is a battle between opposing lawyers in which "winning" the case becomes the major goal. Technical rules control the admission of evidence, as the rules for football or basketball guide how the game is played.

What is the thinking behind this adversary system? One law professor has said: "The underlying hope is that if the law permits the lawyer-gladiators to make the fight, out of the clash and clang of their legal or factual battling the rights of the case will appear and justice be done."

But does it work that way? Legal scholars point out that the adversary system sounds good in theory. But to make it operate perfectly both parties should have the money to pay for thorough investigations. They would need the same good or bad luck in finding witnesses and securing evidence. They should have equal skill in presenting the evidence and organizing their case. Yet it rarely happens that the two sides are ever roughly equal in these things.

Roscoe Pound, a dean of the Harvard Law School, once commented that the adversary system "leads the most conscientious judge to feel that he is merely to decide the contest . . . according to the rules of the game, not to search independently for truth and justice." He added that the lawyers act more like professional football coaches, out to win for their side. Expert witnesses called to testify are less concerned with the facts than with scoring points for the side that pays them. The system, he went on, "prevents the trial court from restraining the bullying of witnesses and creates a general dislike, if not fear, of the witness function which impairs the administration of justice."

Clearly, the adversary method assumes that both sides will be equally matched in means, material, and skill. But that is seldom the case. What happens is that the victory often goes to the powerful rather than to the party who is in the right.

Is that justice? The system's critics do not believe it is. Whom does the system benefit? Usually the rich and the powerful, say the critics. They can buy the expert counsel necessary to win. The system seems the creation of people who love to fight, not those who love peace. For it requires that all persons who must go to law to settle differences should behave as enemies. The courtroom is the arena for combat between adversaries.

Under the adversary system each side is not obliged to

present all it knows, but only its own "best case." Information is avoided or suppressed as eagerly as it is sought. Priority is given to selective representation and misrepresentation in such a win-or-lose trial procedure.

Rarely is the fighting in a court trial fair. Those who can pay for the services of the best lawyers are likely to win. It is doubtful that winning a trial and winning justice are the same thing. "In the justice game," Gerry Spence, a highly successful trial lawyer, has written,

the mismatch between opponents is usually . . . ridiculous. If we are maimed by a drunk in the most ordinary automobile accident, rarely will we be taking on the drunk himself; rather, one or more of the world's great insurance companies will secretly be standing in for the drunk, supplying him with the best lawyers, the best witnesses, the best defense money can buy. If your spouse and child are burned to death in a defective automobile manufactured by Ford, that company can call upon its 14,000 engineers who, by sophisticated experiments especially conducted for the case, can prove in court that their cars walk on water, and it can tap at will its resources of $15 billion or more to buy the great trial lawyers and hire the renowned experts necessary to defeat your claim. Usually, by the time any wrongfully injured person comes to court he will be out of work and deeply in debt and desperate to feed his family. But to get justice he must take on one of the great corporations of the world and win—not only with the jury, but with the judges as well. . . .

Because the adversary system is by definition either-or, no third person may enter the contest without being placed, by himself or herself or by the court, "for" one side or the other. There is no room for an impartial witness at the trial court (except at the appellate level, where most cases never arrive). So an expert witness is not called for an objective view, for disinterested testimony wherever it may lead. No, an expert witness is called *by* a side, or *for* a side. He or she is interviewed in advance and chosen only if the testimony will support the side that calls him or her, or provide ammunition against the other side. What are such experts but partisans? Yet juries are expected to decide which has most convincingly called the other a liar. Is it impossible that truth may lie somewhere in between? Or be something that neither side has testified to? Not with a win-or-lose system, say its critics.

One of the essential aspects of the adversary system is the cross-examination. The opposing lawyers question the other side's witnesses after direct examination by their own lawyer has taken place, and they attempt to uncover material hidden or underdeveloped. The witness's motives, prejudices, knowledge, and power of memory and description are analyzed by this means. By cross-examination the lawyer tries to obtain helpful testimony and to discredit harmful testimony. The lawyer wants to demean the harmful witness, to cast doubt on his or her truthfulness, to lay the basis for objecting to his or her "incompetent" testimony.

Can truth be the goal for such cross-examination? It is victory the lawyers are after. Manuals of instruction make that clear. Such books, to quote one of them, "advise the lawyer that he has the duty to give the jury, if possible, a false impression of testimony unfavorable to his side."

When a witness is apparently honest, and his or her evidence damaging, the lawyers may twist the cross-examination to suggest that the entire testimony has no importance. One professor of law has put it bluntly: "It is 'ethical' for defense counsel to cross-examine a prosecution witness to make him appear to be inaccurate or untruthful, even when the defense attorney knows that the witness is testifying accurately or truthfully." Supreme Court Justice Byron White held that if defense counsel can "confuse a witness, even a truthful one, or make him appear at a disadvantage, unsure or indecisive, that will be his normal course." Thus the witness stand has come to be known as "the slaughterhouse of reputations."

Character assassination is a weapon used not only by the defense. The record shows it is employed just as commonly by plaintiffs in civil suits and by the prosecution in criminal cases—or wherever cross-examination comes into play and the goal is winner take all.

Reagan's Legions of Nominees P His Own Stamp on the Judiciary

By STEVEN V. ROBERTS

WASHINGTON

ALL summer, 29 of President Reagan's nominations to the F...
languish...

During the first term of the ...
tration, normal attrition will p
more than 100 judgeships. In ad
ber of older ...

Psychologist's Expert Testimon Called Unscienti

...tional Effect Seen in Ruling On Black Judicial Candidates

— SMOTHERS

...CKSBURG, Miss. —
ruling that judges we
...ssippi in a discrimi
...s changing the racia
...udiciary here. And
...nded in the Voting F
...g may affect many
...s that elect trial ju

...e decision held th
...s at the state and
...ions for governo
...ol board, are su
...rimination

...ring the
Federa
...es, acc

...anges are already
...diciary, most

But defenders say critics ...aggerate the problems.

/ DANIEL GOLEMAN

Broader Curbs Sought On Challenging Jurors

By LINDA GREENHOUS
Special to The Ne

WASHINGTON, Dec. 30 — T...
after the Supreme C...
stricted the ab...
create a...

...OGISTS and ...

...ed Trials Stir Fears of Wrongful Executio

W H. MALCOLM

...ase of a former death
...atedly found to have
...nvicted, underlines a
...edged danger in the
...ial system: the virtual
...metimes executing inno-

...f the death penalty say
...sibility should be suffi-
...w executions. Its propo-
...ongful executions are pos-
...eir minuscule number is
...by the larger good of social
...and deterrence. They re-
...releases as proof that the
... system works, eventually
...at its mistakes.
...ues are expected
...tly later this month.
...Legislature again c
...g Gov. Mario M. Cuom
...reinstituting the death p
...ected close vote reflects
...onal struggle over the

Critics respond that Mr. Richard-son's reprieve, like the eventual re-lease of many innocents from death row, had nothing to do with his guilt or innocence. With the Supreme Court decision in Furman v. Georgia, Mr. Richardson's death sentence, and 557 others, was automatically commuted to life imprisonment. Otherwise, he would have been executed before the grave faults in his trial were uncov-ered.

Since 1976, 38 states have reinsti-tuted the death penalty under the court's stricter guidelines.
...cutions have b...
than ...

financed legal defenses. "With Chief Justice Rehnquist calling for a speed-up in death penalty appeals," said Mr. Tabak, "I'm afraid we'll be executing even more innocent people."

Perjury Often a Factor

In their study, Professors Radelet and Bedau found the most common reason for erroneous conviction was perjury by prosecution witnes...
Others included false ...
pression h...

...ties because the advantage
...the disadvantages. So I am
...the death penalty because
...society more than any ot
...penalty could."

Leigh Dingerson, direc
...tional Coalition to Aboli
...Penalty, disagree...
...few inno...

Overturned Murder Conviction Spotlights Da...

By PETER APPLEBOME
Special to The New York Times

DALLAS, March 4 — For the second time in five years, justice in Dallas is under a national spotlight. First it was Lenell Geter, a young black engineer who was freed from prison in 1984 after being given a life sentence for an armed robbery he did not commit. Now it is Randall Dale Adams, who nar-rowly escaped being executed 12 years mously overturned this week, murder conviction that was unani-after his trial.

Legal experts say wrongful convic-tions can and do happen elsewhere. But not many lawyers in Texas are sur-prised that two of the most publicized legal nightmares of recent years hap-pened here.

"The feeling of the prosecutors in Dallas back then was that we can't be wrong, that basically we're gods in de-creeing who shall live and who shall die, who goes to prison and who goes free," said Randy Schaffer, the attorney who successfully Mr. Adams ...

dicted parts of their testimony. Officer Turko substantially changed her story in the course of the proceedings.

A Legal Break in 1979

When the defense tried to recall sur-prise witnesses presented on the last day of the trial, Mr. Mulder said they had left the state. In fact, they were in a Dallas motel room. When the defense tried to present a full picture of Mr. Harris's juvenile crime record, it was ruled inadmissible.

Mr. Adams's one prior legal break came in 1979, when the United States Supreme Court overturned his death sentence because of the way the jury was selected. Although District Attor-...
...playing football — occa-...
...ly lead to the death of innocent people. We don't give up these activi-

ney Henry Wade had vowed to the case to get the death penalt he never so. Instead, at his Gov. Bill Clements commute tence to life over Mr. Adar tions, avoiding a new trial.

Mr. Bruder, who succes sented Mr. Adams before Court, said the Adams c in extreme form, the n prosecutor's office and as a whole in the 1970'

"You can't have a t that is overzealous who are willing to said. "It's one and ya It's yin and ya prosecutors can'

...e Court o Of the tota four killed ag killed again former Dea mitted suic

Cases in Texas and Florida raise a specter that haunts many.

...nd political issue of taking a life in ret-...
...bution for taking a life. A fundamen-
...al but often overlooked fact is that the
...constitutional guarantee of a fair trial
...does not always guarantee an accurate
...verdict.

...week, a Florida judge blamed
...duct and perjured
...ion of

Death Penalty Law in Illino

SPRINGFIELD, Ill., May 1 (AP) —
...nois's
...held by
...1979.

Federal judge struck down the death ...casualty law in Illinois Monday, raising ...doubts about the fate of 121 prisoners ...repre attention...the state's death row.
...Hous Morris's documentary which was...
...line," federal District Judge Harold Baker
...decide that the 1977 law gives prosecu-
...too much discretion in deciding

Judge
case of
the dea
in 1980
Mr.

...ging, fitness for chil
...nsequences of a physical

☞ # 15 ☜

Juries and Judges

AT THE HEART of the legal system is trial by jury. A group of citizens—usually twelve in number though it can be six at times—hears the case, with the guidance of a judge. The judge must not try to dominate the jury or to take over its functions. When presentation of the case is completed, the judge tells the jury the legal rules that are to govern their deliberations. The judge also reviews the evidence presented in the trial, puts it in logical form, and tells the jury if there are any doubtful areas they need be aware of. Then the jury goes out to deliberate in secret upon the case. When the jury comes to a decision (by unanimous vote, typically), it returns to the courtroom and announces its verdict. It does not explain or justify its verdict.

Whatever disagreements, controversy, pressure, and

compromise may have occurred among the jurors during the weighing of evidence and exhibits and during the judge's instructions remain a secret. Sometimes a jury ignores the judge's instruction as to what the law is in the particular case. It may not understand them. Or it decides against both facts and the law because that is the mood of the community and the expression of the jurors' own prejudices. (Examples are the cases of white defendants who, before spectators, killed black people in the South and were declared not guilty by the jury.) On the other hand, a jury may refuse to abide by a harsh or unfair law when its own conscience, its own sense of justice, its compassion for another human being, leads it to go against the court's instructions. So juries can and do nullify the law at times. Not often, however, for most juries do not know they have that power. No one tells them.

In a criminal case, which is what concerns us here, the verdict is always in favor of either the state or the accused. A jury verdict acquitting the accused in a criminal case cannot be set aside by the judge, even when the judge thinks it was clearly unreasonable.

What does trial by jury in a criminal case mean? It means that before a person's life or freedom or reputation is taken from him or her by the state, that person's guilt, and the degree of it, must have been made clear to the ordinary citizen—to twelve men and women speaking with a single voice. Jurors, unlike lawyers and judges, are not professionally trained or experienced in the law. They are ordinary men and women who take on the task for just one occasion. Their education, occupation, and income are generally average. They do their work in secret and rarely discuss in public the trial they have heard or how they reached the verdict. Judges usually advise them not to discuss the trial. Many legal authorities praise the jury system lavishly, calling it "a safeguard to liberty," "the glory of the law," "a vital institution." They believe that the jury system is the best way to investigate the truth.

But others take a somewhat different view. Jerome Frank, a federal judge, described it as "antiquated . . . and inherently absurd—so much so that no lawyer, judge, scholar, prescription clerk, cook or mechanic in a garage would ever think for a moment of employing that method for determining the facts in any situation that concerned him." He went on to say, "A better instrument could scarcely be imagined for achieving uncertainty, capriciousness, lack of uniformity, disregard of former decisions— utter unpredictability." Leonard Levy, noted legal scholar, wrote, "A jury is essentially a court of public opinion, often synonymous with public prejudice."

A trial by jury is supposed to be impartial. It is hardly likely that it will be, embedded as it is in the adversary system. Lawyers try to select as jurors those people who will be most influenced by the emotional theatrics of the lawyer's performance. Most lawyers try to sniff out bias in favor of their client and to eliminate any potential jurors whose bias goes against their client. If bias isn't detectable, they try to create it in their favor. Many considerations enter the choice of jurors: how a person looks, occupation, sex, dress, age, physical disability, gait. . . . Lately, more sophisticated methods of jury selection have come into use, with lawyers buying advice from experts who apply to jury selection the principle of marketing research. The result: The side with the bigger bucks has the more favorable jury.

Trial by jury as against trial by a judge alone is thought to be more democratic. Through the jury the public itself takes part in the trial (although fewer than one percent of the population ever serve on a jury). A dozen people, it is claimed, are better able to judge motives and weigh evidence than a single person. A jury shares in the common sense of the community and in its ethical standards. But if the jury's main function is to determine the facts, then, as we have seen, the adversary procedure works to prevent precisely that.

Lawyers have their eye not only on the bias of a perspective juror but on that person's ignorance of the class of facts he or she is supposed to determine. Anyone with experience or knowledge in the matter at issue is ruled out. Jurors selected usually have few qualifications for fact finding.

A great many cases never reach a jury for decision. The process called plea bargaining takes place instead. It is defended as a necessary measure to speed the course of justice. With the rise in crime and the increasing pressure on the courts, a heavy backlog of cases delays justice. So in about 90 percent of criminal cases, a plea bargain is made.

What is a plea bargain? It's a deal struck privately, with the court's approval, between the accused and his or her lawyer on one hand and the prosecutor on the other. Often the prosecutor takes what is actually a single accusation and breaks it into several parts, charging each as a separate offense. Or the prosecutor adds a conspiracy count. Sometimes he or she may overcharge, calling an offense a felony when it is only a misdemeanor. The accused, seeing himself or herself in even greater trouble than he or she thought, is overwhelmed by the danger of a heavy sentence if convicted and is pushed into settling for a lesser charge. If the accused gives up the right to trial by pleading guilty to one charge out of the many, or to a lesser misdemeanor rather than a felony, then the prosecutor will drop the other charges. When such a bargain is made, the case is concluded and the sentence handed down. It cannot be appealed. The outcome means the state has saved the time and expense of a trial, the prosecutor is spared the trouble of building his or her case and perhaps losing it, and the defense attorney has been paid for very little work.

A study of plea bargaining in drug-related cases during 1988–89 was made in New York City. It showed it is not uncommon for a defendant charged with a crime that could carry a maximum of twenty-five years in jail to plead guilty to a reduced charge and, in the case of a first offense, to receive a sentence ranging from five years' probation to six months in jail.

Most drug defendants are allowed to plead guilty to lesser charges because the justice system cannot handle the rising flood of drug felony arrests. The plea bargain, said the head of the private Crime Commission of New York, "doesn't send a strong message to drug dealers." A spokesman for the Legal Aid Society suggested a better alternative

to the present system is to spend the money to make
treatment available to drug addicts. The way it now stands,
he added, we've "taken a person off the street who is a
junkie, and we've made him a felon. What have we accom-
plished? We've jammed our system and haven't solved the
drug problem."

Whatever the crime, the accused, if guilty, comes out
ahead, with a lesser punishment. If the accused is guilty,
he or she receives punishment less than the law would
have applied as the result of a conviction in a trial. But if
the accused is really innocent, he or she is a loser. In that
situation, the accused is punished without a chance to
prove his or her innocence before a jury.

With white-collar criminals, plea bargaining is used
"with bargain-basement abandon," as one writer put it,
speaking of prosecutions of high government officials for
wrongdoing. Officials who violate their oath of office and
the Constitution often get off with lighter sentences than
an adolescent car thief.

Some critics of the legal system make the point that it
is judges, not juries, who really decide cases. The jury does
not hear a case unless the trial judge permits the case to
go to trial. When all the evidence is in, the judge decides
whether the party has presented a sufficient case for the
jury to hear. If the judge determines it has not, the case
is dropped. Even after a jury in a civil case has come to a
decision, if the judge doesn't like it, he or she has the
authority to set it aside and to order a new trial for whatever
reason he or she may give. What controls the court is what
the judge says controls it.

In criminal cases, when the liberty and perhaps the life

of the accused is at stake, a jury's decision to acquit must stand. The accused cannot be ordered to stand trial again because of the constitutional provision against placing a person in double jeopardy.

So judges have great power. They interpret the laws and apply them. Although they are often viewed as superior beings above the common run of citizens, they are, of course, human. They inevitably make decisions that express their personal view of the world. In doing so, they intervene in almost every aspect of our daily life, from the trivial to the tragic.

Judges are sworn to uphold the U.S. Constitution, which spells out certain broad principles of moral justice. It states that no person may be deprived of life, liberty, or property without "due process of law." That is meant to assure fairness, consistency, equality, impartiality, justice. The Constitution also guarantees certain broad freedoms— such as freedom of speech and religion. It guarantees certain broad rights as well, such as the right not to be subjected to unreasonable searches and seizures, the right to an impartial trial, and the right of all citizens to equal protection of the law.

How the system of justice works under the Constitution depends in great part upon the role of judges, as we have seen. Who are the men and women who possess these powers? They are ordinary mortals, neither saints nor devils. The large majority are white Protestant males, middle-aged, coming from well-to-do families. They have few or no ties to the poor, to minorities, or to the victims of social injustice.

Appointed to the bench, judges do not shed their upbringing, their experience, their tastes and prejudices. What they have become in life is the reason for their selection. Presidents appoint them to the federal bench, subject to the approval of the Senate, and they are expected to reflect the chief executive's interests. Once in office, a president's choice may act differently from what the president had expected. President Theodore Roosevelt appointed Oliver Wendell Holmes, Jr., whose decisions disappointed the president. President Dwight D. Eisenhower picked Earl Warren to be chief justice because he thought Warren was a conservative like himself. Sadly he confessed how wrong he'd been.

By the time President Ronald Reagan finished his second term in the White House, he had appointed over half the nation's 744 federal judges, including three to the Supreme Court, as well as a new chief justice. About 90 percent of the Reagan judges are male, white, and Republican, and 65 percent are Protestant. About two-thirds had a net worth of $200,000 to $1 million. Nearly half had been prosecutors. As private lawyers, a great many had represented corporate clients. All of Reagan's choices were thoroughly screened to make sure their political philosophy agreed with his.

More federal appointees under Democrats tend to be Catholics, Jews, or lower-status Protestants; Democrats tend to appoint more blacks and women than do Republicans.

A Judicature Society study of how federal judges are evaluated found that a strong link exists between politics and judging. Candidates for judgeships or their sponsors contribute to political parties and candidates and have ties to important senators and congressional committees. It is not to be wondered at if judges decide cases according to their political obligations. If they come from the upper reaches of society or have served the powerful, how many are likely to do anything to weaken that power or go against its desires?

Under the adversary system the judge is seen as an "umpire" between two contestants and, in theory, impartial. She or he makes no independent investigation of the case and has no means for doing so. She or he applies the law to the facts as each side urges them. The same evidence that may be convincing to one judge may be utterly absurd to another. Yet the judge's decision becomes the law. When a judge decides a case, she or he is making law. It is the judge's decisions that will be enforced.

There is evidence for how personal differences among judges affect their decisions. A study was made in the criminal courts of New York City to see how the "personal equation" shapes justice. The data gathered on similar classes of cases showed that out of 566 persons charged with intoxication, one judge found 565 guilty and 1 not guilty, or less than 1 percent. But a colleague, handling 673 persons charged with the same offense, found 142 guilty and discharged 531, or nearly 79 percent. Or take disorderly conduct: one judge discharged 18 percent, another, 54 percent. Sentencing, too, covered a wide range. Judge A fined 85 percent and suspended sentence on 7 percent, whereas on the same charge Judge B fined 34 percent and suspended sentence on 59 percent.

Those judges in a municipal court obviously differed
mightily on how they saw the facts and how they felt about
the human side of people's behavior. The same happens
all the way up the judicial ladder to the very top. In a
recent session of the U.S. Supreme Court, of sixty-six decisions handed down, twenty-nine were decided by the
majority of a single vote—and often with vigorous dis-
senting opinions. Juries are required to bring in unanimous verdicts, but Supreme Court decisions can be made
by a mere majority.

Overburdened Prisons Po

A Crisis for Massachus

The 'Tough-Guy' Drug

It's Nothing to Brag Ab

By Tom Wicker

NCORD, Mass., July 8 — A stable-
nell sours the air in the basement
of the Massachusetts
Institution at C
that

NEW YORK — With m
San po

uantities. U.S. Customs alor
i 24 metric tons of cocain
ainst only 5.2 metric tons i
Yet in South Florida, the p
caine has fallen to $9,000 a
out $60,000 in 1982. This c
y if the supply has increas
greater amounts seized.

all of the cocaine, heroin
a coming into the Uni
seized, moreover, the dr
ould offer a bazaar of n
bstances — amphetamin
s, PCP, LSD, many opia
nts, alcohol, and on and
ment rejected in the H
have increased taxes
es and wine to pay for
ogram. Now there is
two most abused
alcohol and nicotine
ating people against
ut what politician
I raising taxes part
a's favorite addictive
he New York Times.

o Is Executed, and Where

ath Sentences
Carried Out

ince capital punishment was
einstituted in 1976.

Race of Prisoners On Death Row

Black 40% / White 52% / Other 2% / Hispanic 6%

Race of Those Executed

Black 39% / White 56% / Hispanic

ison at a Crossroads:
o Punish or to Counsel

By ANDREW H. MA

icials and criminologists are
he operations of an unusual
prison that emphasizes re-
over retribution.
al debate began in special
earings at Annapolis Dec

and ex
Cali
psycho
progra
Institut
mates

Capital Punishment Is Po
But So Are Its Alternativ

ives of Women in Prison

By JOHN J. O'CONNOR

of Fox Broadcasting's more
r contributions to prime-time
has been the series called
in Prison," a sitcom
d with lovably tough, wise-
good-time gals who seem-
life behind bars a bit of a
e laugh track had a pro-
male heartiness, heavy on
har, har" kind of guffaw
o mud-wrestling matches.
vers found the incarcera-
hilarious in their un-
garity. Those same view-
ke a look at tonight's edi-
rents" on Channel 13 at
arlene Sanders as host,
m examines "Women

y Henry Singer, thi-
ay visits New
ion fo

time for possession of and conspiracy
to sell drugs. She notes that "drugs
was my escape" while living in a
torious housing project in Patters
Lisa is visited by her 13-year-
daughter, who, having to pass muste
for entry to the prison, is treated like
a suspect herself.

Pat, formerly hooked on heroin and
cocaine, is serving four years for
theft. The thievery, she says, was
"just a mechanical thing; I had to go
out and make my money or I'd be
sick." She is now fighting to retain
custody of her two sons.

Joy, convicted of assault, has already lost three of her five children to
adoption and admits that she is not
sure that she will be able to ta
of the other two when
fact, she isn't
care of

COLM

ocuted Alton Waye 10
raping

The American Way: Guns and Death

By ANDREW H. MALCO

Someone in the U
States dies from a gu
every 16 minutes.

Often what most
guishes these killings
casual nature. The gu
here was a surplus
revolver from th
mento Police De
bought by a groce
his 19-year-old

In a society increasing
violent crime th
flict

A gun used by a
woman to kill

'Club Fed'

hy Execution is Dead Wrong

How many James Richardsons does it take to
nge an attitude? It is a deadly serious question.
James Richardson, a Florida migrant worker,
s sentenced to death in 1968 after being convicted
poisoning his seven children. But he was saved
m execution by the Supreme Court's 1972 deci-
n striking down state capital punishment laws.

This week he went free after a judge ruled his
nviction tainted by prosecutorial misconduct and
rjured testimony. It now appears that someone
se killed the Richardson children.

Mr. Richardson was the second man in two
nths to win freedom after it became clear that he

According to Michael R
Florida specialist on capital
been 30 cases since 1972 in
victed and sentenced to dea
after the state admitted a m

The question is real a
James Richardsons or Ra
take to change a nation's at
ishment? No one has yet
deterrent value for the dea
function is to satisfy a pri
tion. But is that sort of sati
30 innocent people? Or ever

Death is the only final
punishment. As the Richa
humans an

Where the
White-Col
Inmate Sta

By DAVID S. WILSON

HERE are no cells or perimete
eral Prison Camp at Lompoc,
convicted of insider stock

☞ 16 ☜

Prison

THE CORRECTIONAL SYSTEM in many places is in very bad shape. The jails and prisons are grossly overcrowded and poorly financed; the facilities obsolete; rehabilitation programs inadequate and unenlightened; and staffs undermanned and poorly trained. Thoroughgoing reform is needed.

Those findings were not made yesterday, but over twenty years ago, by the President's Crime Commission. Has much been done since then? Once, not so long ago, prison movies that aroused sympathy for inmates portrayed as victims of sadistic guards were very popular. No more. The public has become too cynical, so sick of a relentless diet of crime news that it demands only more toughness, not less. Calling for retribution, not reform, is an easy way for politicians to get votes.

Back in the 1950s, Maryland opened an unusual prison that emphasized rehabilitation, or helping prisoners, instead of punishing them. The state legislature funded it at a time when people believed prison inmates could, with help, become law-abiding citizens. It stressed psychotherapy and education to change behavior. It used a system of work-release, furloughs, parole, and parole officers. With good behavior and progress in treatment, the inmate could move stage by stage to earlier release.

Furloughs for prisoners became a heated issue in the 1988 presidential campaign. But a study of such temporary release from custody found that of the 53,000 inmates in federal and state prisons given more than 200,000 furloughs in 1987, only a few did any harm. The program is generally considered highly successful, according to the study made by Contact Center, a nonprofit criminal justice information clearinghouse in Lincoln, Nebraska. Furloughs exist now in the prison systems of every state and in the federal system, as well. They affect nearly 10 percent of the total prison population of over half a million.

Furloughs are usually granted near the end of a prisoner's sentence. They permit inmates to look for work and re-enter their communities. They are also given to enable inmates to get medical care, enter religious or treatment programs, or enjoy shopping or recreation. Who is given furloughs is determined by several careful standards within the prison and by the views of the victims of crime, community leaders, and local law-enforcement officials.

By the late 1980s, some critics were attacking such special programs and prisons. They said furloughs conflicted with a view of justice as proper punishment for the crime committed. "If you do the crime, you do the time." These critics spoke for people who no longer felt sympathy for those who end up in prison.

The decade of the 1980s ended with more than half a million inmates in federal and state prisons. It was the most explosive growth in the prison population in the nation's history. Five percent of the total inmates are women: 27,000 of them are in prisons around the nation. Their number has jumped 140 percent in the last decade. No one is sure why that increase has occurred.

Young people in trouble with the law—some of them not yet in their teens—can be confined in three main ways: in adult jails, in local juvenile detention centers, and in state institutions often called training schools. On any given day, about 40,000 youths are in confinement at one level or another. Although a federal law of 1974 prohibits putting children in the same jail with adults, about twenty states still do not comply with the law. About 60,000 juveniles wind up in adult jails each year. About 415,000 youths spend some time in public detention centers. Because of the jammed juvenile justice system, the detention centers are badly overcrowded in most cities. They were originally meant to be holding places while the young people's cases were being processed. But many became places of punishment. The dangerous youths are packed in with the others, making the system a breeding ground for young criminals in much the same way the prisons are for older criminals. About 65,000 are confined in training schools, where young people considered the most dangerous are sent for terms of usually a year or more.

Within the juvenile justice system there is a split over how to handle young offenders. At one end of the spectrum are states like Massachusetts and Utah that have developed such programs as group homes, foster care, and other alternatives to jailing. In New York State, the Vera Institute of Justice, a private nonprofit organization, developed the Court Employment Project (CEP). It is an agency to which judges can sentence convicted young adults who would otherwise spend substantial time behind bars because probation could not adequately control them. Employing them in its own work crews, CEP requires them to attend remedial classes at its on-site school. It surrounds them with required and productive activitiy throughout the day. And finally, by bringing absconders back to the sentencing judges for imprisonment, CEP has been able to assure the courts that the high-risk youth sentenced to its program will not go unsupervised.

Judges like the program. Under CEP young people are not put into prisons that will make them tougher when they get out. The program's threat of immediate jailing for failure to comply with supervision holds great promise for turning young offenders away from crime.

At the opposite end are California and some other western states that are tending toward "locking them all up." According to Ellen Schall, Commissioner of the New York City Department of Juvenile Justice, "If we give up on these kids now, we're guaranteeing ourselves a generation of lost kids who we'll just have to deal with as adults later on."

The percentage of Americans in prison has more than doubled since 1970. In 1970 there were about 110 prisoners for every 100,000 residents. By 1988 there were 228 for every 100,000. (The United States confines more of its citizens than any other Western nation.) Yearly prison construction costs have climbed to more than $1 billion at the same time that the nation's prisons have become desperately overcrowded.

Was this rise in imprisonment effective? Was it affordable? Such questions and doubts about the answers helped introduce experiments with alternatives. It was urged that we reconsider the harsher sentencing plans developed in recent years. Or that we try confining certain lesser offenders at home with electronic monitoring. But the widespread fear of crime would seem to make a major shift in imprisonment unlikely. In fact, the movement is the other way. New federal sentencing guidelines are projected to increase the prison population by 21 percent by the year 1992. They call for tougher penalties and virtually eliminate probation for most federal offenders.

As prison costs skyrocket, people begin to realize we can't build our way out of crime. The price tag on a new prison ranges from $50,000 to $75,000 a cell. Keeping a prisoner in a state or federal prison costs from $12,000 to $30,000 a year. The National Council on Crime and Delinquency pointed out that in 1988 we were putting about 750 more inmates in prison each week than we released. Half the people were in there for property crime. How many of these people, the council asked, did we want to lock up and for what periods of time?

In the last part of the 1980s many counties in forty states introduced programs to provide the courts with choices between probation and imprisonment. One option calls for intensive supervised probation programs, most of which include payment to victims and required service of some kind to the community. Several states are experimenting with electronic monitoring devices worn by the offender, mostly for use in house arrests.

Officials worry that alternative penalty programs might become a more lenient way to treat white, middle-class offenders. Convicted white-collar criminals, such as Wall Street's Ivan Boesky and several convicted government officials, serve their relatively brief terms in federal minimum-security camps, where the harshest visible restriction may be a Keep Off the Grass sign.

Why should such camps be appropriate for people convicted of such white-collar crimes as fraud, embezzlement, forgery, corruption, counterfeiting, and violation of regulations? It can be argued that white-collar criminals do far more harm to society than do inmates in the maximum-security prisons who are convicted of violent crime. Nevertheless, federal officials believe that as the prison population grows and costs soar, the country may rely more and more on the minimum-security camps. They cost only about half as much to operate as the more secure prisons.

What about the future? Some experts see hopeful signs in a population change. Since the early 1980s the number of young men in the most crime-prone age group—the late teens and early twenties—has been dropping. On the other hand, the explosive growth in violent and drug-related crime has heated public anger enough to curb tendencies toward a leveling off of imprisonment.

Not long ago the state of Washington issued a Help Wanted! flier for an experienced hangman. State officials said they were having trouble filling the job. It needed someone with the scientific skills to handle math, momentum, and distance. The person had to be able to assess the height and weight of the doomed prisoner, the proper drop from the platform, and obviously, the right knot. "We don't want this to be any more unpleasant than it has to be," said a prison warden. "We certainly don't want a decapitation."

No, decapitation would be an outmoded way of carrying out the death penalty. Today, hanging and shooting are the most common methods of execution worldwide. In the United States, electrocution and lethal injections of poison are also used. But, once upon a time, convicted criminals were flogged, impaled, boiled in oil, broken on the wheel, and finally sawn in half. The English favored drawing and quartering. The condemned was hanged, dismembered while still alive, then decapitated and quartered. The fragments of the corpse were put on public display to reinforce the message that bad things would happen to you for committing a crime.

Crimes that merit capital punishment were once far more numerous than they are now. We no longer execute people because we dislike their politics or their religion. Back around 1800, the English code listed over two hundred crimes punishable by death. To steal a turnip, be seen with Gypsies, poach game, or cut down a tree could get you killed. In colonial America, Massachusetts law provided death for blasphemy, idolatry, or witchcraft. Women accused of sorcery were hanged in the Salem witchcraft trials, and one old man was crushed to death between heavy stones. In the South, the death penalty was also used to protect slavery. To shelter a fugitive slave or incite slaves to rebellion could result in the death penalty.

Two reasons are usually given to justify the death penalty. One: The risk of execution prevents people from committing murder. Two: Those who murder deserve to die. "An eye for an eye . . ." But critics ask, What evidence is there that fear of death stops criminals from committing violent crimes? Most murders involve people who know one another and are the outcome of passionate and powerful feelings of the moment. In such situations no one stops to ponder the possible sentence of death.

Then, too, there is certain knowledge that innocent victims are wrongfully convicted of murder and executed. What amends can be made for taking that life? It is argued, however, that the economic cost to society of confining a murderer to prison for life overrides the occasional mistake. Even that cold calculation of life and death in terms of money has been disputed. Recent statistics show that the dollar cost to society for multiple trials and hearings in death-penalty cases—they consume on the average more than seven years and cost more than a million dollars—usually exceeds the cost of housing the prisoner for the rest of his or her life. As Supreme Court Justice Thurgood Marshall once remarked ironically, it would be cheaper to shoot the defendant at the time of his arrest.

Probably the first public protest against capital punishment was made by an Italian, the Marquis Beccaria, in 1764, in his *Essay on Crime and Punishment.* Enlightened Americans like Dr. Benjamin Rush (1745–1813) of Philadelphia took up the cry against the death penalty, and Quakers helped persuade the Pennsylvania legislature in 1798 to abolish it in all cases except first-degree murder. But other states continued to execute horse thieves, pickpockets, burglars, and in some cases, even children accused of showing disrespect to their parents.

Gradually, death for crimes other than murder and sometimes rape was eliminated. In 1846, Michigan was the first state to abolish it altogether. About a hundred years later, only eight other states had followed suit. Though the number of executions had dropped, there was no sustained movement against the death penalty. In the late 1950s a private New York committee for abolition was formed, and in 1965 that state ended the death penalty. Over the years, the pendulum of public opinion swung back and forth—now for abolition of the death penalty, now against.

Opponents in the 1960s began to argue that the death penalty was outright illegal, charging it violated the Eighth Amendment's prohibition against "cruel and unusual punishment." The debate heated up until in 1967 the Supreme Court refused to allow any more executions until it was prepared to decide the issue one way or the other. It meant a moratorium on all executions. Not for another ten years—until 1977—did any one of the hundreds of prisoners on death rows actually die.

In 1972 the Supreme Court struck down all existing death penalty legislation because it held that it was being applied in an "arbitrary and capricious way," and as such, it constituted "cruel and unusual punishment." This decision, most opponents of capital punishment thought, would effectively end the death penalty. But that proved wishful thinking on their part. Within a few years many states enacted new death laws to provide standards for juries and judges to follow in determining the sentence in capital cases or in more narrowly defining the crimes for which the penalty would be imposed. In 1976, the Supreme Court reviewed what had happened. While declaring illegal any mandatory death sentences, it upheld several laws providing standards for imposing the death penalty. Six months later Gary Gilmore in Utah was the first on death row to be legally executed in nearly a decade.

In the United States, in 1989, there were about two thousand people on death row—one of the largest death-row populations in the world. In most states that retain the death penalty it is reserved for first-degree murder and is discretionary. The death sentence is usually imposed for murder committed during the course of an additional serious offence, such as rape or armed robbery.

The death sentence is appealed automatically to the highest state court and can be carried up to the U.S. Supreme Court for review of constitutional issues. Many states did revise death penalty statutes to bring them into line with constitutional standards. But Amnesty International and other civil liberties groups maintain there is still ample evidence that "the death penalty is disproportionately carried out against minorities, the poor, and the mentally ill."

The facts show that while blacks make up 12 percent of the population, they represent 41 percent of prisoners on death row. Black defendants, particularly in the South, which has the highest execution rate, have often been convicted by all-white juries. In 1987, 86 percent of U.S. prisoners on death row had been convicted of killing whites. Forty-five of the ninety-eight prisoners executed between January 1987 and May 1988 were black or Hispanic, and 98 percent of them had been convicted of killing whites.

Very often defendants in capital crimes are from the ranks of the poor. The courts assign them Legal Aid lawyers who are often inexperienced and ill-fitted to handle capital cases and extremely limited in their resources.

Human rights scholars point out that the United States acts contrary to international standards when it executes juveniles. International standards maintain that boys and girls under eighteen at the time they committed their crimes should not be executed. Yet in the spring of 1989 the United States had thirty-one juvenile offenders on death row.

The experience of the past several years would seem to indicate that the noted lawyer Anthony Amsterdam was right when he said that death penalty laws are enacted "in a form such that they can be applied sparsely and spottily to unhappy minorities whose numbers are so few, whose plight so invisible, and whose persons so unpopular, that society can readily bear to see them suffer torments which would not for a moment be accepted as penalties of general application to the populace."

Bush Crime Proposal Relies

On D...

...w Efforts Developing Against the Hate C...

...DREW H. MALCOLM

...nd of crime is attracting a
...f attention from Congress
...state legislatures, social
...nd a number of police offi-
...d the country.

...e crime — any assault, in-
...or harassment that is due to
...'s race, religion or ethnic
...nd — is emerging as an area
...growing interest because of
...ularly harmful effect on the
...d its tendency to worsen the
...nsions that already grip some
...ities.

...step, the Senate is expected to
...the next two months on a pro-
...Crimes Statistics Act,... Con...

separate from broader categories —
arson, for example, or assault.

"It will take many years of nation...
reporting before we have a meaningf...
data base," said Joan C. Weiss, exec...
tive director of the National Instit...
Against Prejudice and Violence, a...
vate, nonprofit group in Baltim...
"But we need to start right awa...
Americans realize we have a se...
problem with hate crimes."

Experts believe that one reaso...
crime reports are kept artificial...
is that the victim often chooses t...
to himself that his race, say, v...
cause of an assault.

"There is a special dimensio...
crimes that sets them apart fr...
garden-variety assaults," sai...

...reness within police departments
...nities they protect. "It's
...similar to

The Tough Job
Of Teaching Et...

**Harvard's M.B.A.
students find ethics
can get 'murky.'**

By PAUL WILKES /...

Neighbors began c...
family, and some a...
owner of the cannon...
neared. "We put th...
...said.

have condemned this
class Detroit neighbor...
drew McKee, who ha...
Goldman, Sachs and C...
heard in my section was...
is fair, this unfair —...
work for analyzing the...
"When we discussed...

...rning Disabilities and Crime: Struggle to S...

"You've learned helplessness in seven
...tes," Mr. Lavoie said. "Imagine a
...bilities, unable

Poverty Strikes the Children Hardest

ancy, juvenile delinquency and criminal
behavior that are flooding court dockets in
New York City.

Preliminary results of a pilot study con-
...the foundation in Brooklyn
...released several

...ow, to Figure Why the Poor Get P...

By LEONARD...

NEXT month, George Bus...
gin working toward hia...
gentler" America. But I...
the homeless was under...
swept the Northeast and the annua...
frozen-to-death began, raising the...
this is instead becoming a meaner...
ills are inextricably tied to its deepe...
sions.

Why does the United States have...

How Despair Is Engu...
A Generation in New...

...lter behind
...artons on a sub-freezin...

**...ice of Illiteracy Translates
...nto Poverty and Humiliation**

By JOSEPH BERGER

...a Mack nearly always orders a
...burger when she eats in a coffee
...She is not especially fond of ham-
...gers. But she cannot read a menu
...is fairly sure a coffee shop will
...e a hamburger.
...t the supermark...
...ds she recognize
...aghetti, but she
...a soup from toma...

America's Illiterates
First of three articles.

The 51-year-old M...

Brooklyn Students Urge Classes to Curb Bia...

Racial discrimination is a daily ex-
...rience in the halls, classrooms, cafe-
...aying fields of Brooklyn's
...aid last week at

differences, as well as voluntary activities that could help students celebrate
those differences.

"When we understand, then we can
move on," said John E. Brandon, a
...ber of the Mayor's Commission
...his speaking to about
...students at

blacks in New York City increas...
154 percent in 1987 over 198...
Brooklyn District Attorney El...
Holtzman said. Incidents a...
against Hispanic people rose...
percent and against Asian-A...
by 240 percent, she said.

Little Contact Outside So...

...sed almost all of the s...
...anging in a...

☞ 17 ☜

What Can Be Done About It?

WE'VE SEEN that the criminal justice system has not been able to reduce crime. But even if it worked better, it couldn't reduce crime as long as the conditions exist that breed crime. What are these conditions? "Poverty, illness, injustice, idleness, ignorance, human misery and crime go together," wrote the former attorney general Ramsey Clark.

No one claims that by getting rid of poverty, ignorance, poor health, and ugly environments, we will eliminate all crime. But who can doubt it would make a great difference? There are other causes than these, to be sure, and we will talk about them, too. But first, poverty.

The United States has the highest rate of poverty in the industrial world. And the poor are getting poorer. The average family income of the poorest fifth of the nation dropped about 11 percent in the 1980s. This happened while the average family income of the richest fifth rose by about 14 percent. Poverty is in some ways worse than it was a quarter of a century ago. There has been a major redistribution of income—from the lower income families, especially the poorest, toward the most affluent. So the income gap is getting wider.

Most disturbing to the nation is the growth of the so-called "underclass." It is characterized more and more by homelessness, long-term unemployment, high crime rates, and drug and alcohol addiction. City after city sees growing rates of infant mortality, teenage pregnancy, and welfare dependency in their poorest neighborhoods.

Take the neighborhood map of any city—your own—and mark the places where street crime is highest. It will surely be the parts of town where health is bad, where housing is terrible, where education is poor, where unemployment is high, where segregation pens people in, where public transportation fails. It is in the slums and ghettos where security of person and property—a fundamental right—is absent.

Of course poverty does not inevitably cause criminal conduct. In most poor neighborhoods the great majority of citizens are law-abiding. Like anyone else, they want to enjoy a decent quality of life, they want peace and security. Yet their hopes are blighted by the guilty few who prey on the innocent many. Nor does wealth make those who enjoy it resistant to wrongdoing. We have ample proof of how common white-collar crime is, right up to the top of the executive suites. We are no longer able to say that broken homes, absent fathers, poor education, and the like are the sole causes of crime. White-collar criminals in the million-dollar class suffer from fewer of these social conditions, yet they break the law blithely and frequently.

Although poor people (and probably in the same proportion as those better off) have the same tendency toward larceny, their opportunities are much more limited. When a young black man chooses to steal, what else can he do but hold up people in the street or in small shops or break into an apartment? He rarely burglarizes a home in a prosperous neighborhood because his color makes him too visible.

The chances of getting caught are high and the rewards so small that people who try to live off this kind of crime don't do better than workers in low-paying jobs. But they always hope they'll do better than that and will beat the odds against them. It rarely works out that way.

What about the cause of violent crime? Some say that crimes of violence—and war itself—are the inevitable outcome of humankind's aggressive instinct. It is a popular belief that people are naturally aggressive. But has that conviction any foundation in fact? In 1986, a group of behavioral scientists from twelve nations met in Seville, Spain, to pool research on the issue. They included some of the world's leaders from the fields of the natural and social sciences. They declared that there is no scientific basis to the belief that humans are naturally aggressive and warlike. Neither war nor any other violent behavior is genetically programmed into our human nature, they concluded. Humans do not have a "violent brain."

Earl Warren once wrote, "The crime problem is the overdue debt that the country must pay for ignoring for decades the conditions that breed lawlessness." Evidence of the need for social changes that Justice Warren pointed to is all around us. A recent study shows that 40 percent of New York City's 14,000 youngsters in Family Court have learning disabilities. The majority are age seven to seventeen and have failed in school or have dropped out and have been involved in criminal behavior, from robbery and drug dealing to murder. The link between juvenile delinquency and learning disability found in New York has been observed throughout the nation.

People with a learning disability have trouble processing and understanding spoken, written, or visual information. In most cases, the experts say, these people are of average or above average intelligence with a severe neurological handicap that affects perception. So far there is no cure for it, but if children are helped at an early age, they can learn successfully. The young people in the New York study either had not been diagnosed properly or, if diagnosed, had not been given any help in the public schools. Another study, this time of adult offenders, found that at least 60 percent of them had learning disabilities.

What can be done about this? If the community cares enough, it can direct such children to the right agencies for remedial help. But many of the families such children come from do not qualify for Medicaid and are too poor to pay for tutoring sessions. Carrie Rozelle, of the nonprofit Foundation for Children with Learning Disabilities, says, "There is a tremendous growing underclass of kids with nowhere to turn, with no hope and without anyone to care for them or love them. It's a guarantee that all of us are going to have to pay a price if we don't find a way to help these kids."

The movement to reform America's schools has thus far proved long on talk and short on performance. Some schools in some places have made significant improvements, but most schools are still structured the way they were nearly a hundred years ago. The area of the greatest need, the big-city schools, has been largely bypassed. The head of the Carnegie Institution for the Advancement of Teaching, Ernest L. Boyer, has said, "The condition of urban education remains a national disgrace." Thousands of urban students are "crowded into dilapidated buildings and drift unrecognized from class to class."

What makes the picture even grimmer is the failure to focus on the child's early years. There is no national policy for child care and early childhood education. Great numbers of children are fed into a system leading to failure in school and life. (The much-applauded preschool Head Start program still reaches only 20 percent of the eligible children.)

How desperately child care is needed on a nationwide scale can be seen in the fact that more than 65 percent of the mothers of young children now work. Most work not because they like to but because they *have* to. About half the kids who enter first grade nowadays will live in one-parent homes by the time they finish high school. One in five children returns to an empty house after school.

Illiteracy forms another link to crime. The price of being

unable to read and write becomes poverty, and that, in turn, may lead to desperation and crime. There are now about 23 million people in the United States who cannot read labels, cannot read instructions, cannot read maps or signs, cannot count. This number is growing at an alarming rate—and just at the time when the nation needs more workers with higher literacy.

The problem isn't just personal. It's social. In an economy that has shifted from manufacturing to service, businesses cannot find the employees they need. They want clerks, secretaries, bank tellers, repair people. . . . But too many of the applicants who come to them cannot read, write, or add well enough. The New York Telephone Company, for example, tested nearly twenty-three thousand applicants for operator and repair technician jobs; only 14 percent passed.

Those who fail to find work because they cannot meet an employer's standards end up on welfare or drawing unemployment compensation—which costs the government billions of dollars. Some turn to crime. One authority estimates that 60 percent of state and federal prison inmates cannot read above the sixth-grade level.

Digging into the problem, a congressional subcommittee on education and health proposed that all Americans should be able to get schooling from early childhood on and that more students should have a chance to go to college. In today's complex and sophisticated environment, better education for more people is urgently required. Some in Congress believe that just as soldiers returning from World War II were given federal aid for higher education (the GI bill), so should all eligible students today be assured of the same chance. The committee report proposed a longer school year, such as other developed countries provide. (In Japan it is 240 days; here it is 180.) It also urged that schools be kept open nights, weekends, holidays, and summers, so they can be used to meet basic community needs: adult literacy programs, job counseling, drug and alcohol counseling.

The list of changes to be made and failures to be remedied to reduce crime can be extended. Everyone asks: Can the nation afford it?

One answer was given recently by Judge David L. Bazelon, who served for thirty-five years on the U.S. Court of Appeals. He wrote a book about what he called "the losers" of contemporary American society in which he said:

We are confronted today by a class of people being left behind in an increasingly affluent society—the losers in . . . a constant war of all against all and each against the other. We see them—defendants and victims—every day in our criminal justice system. Our society ignores these facts only at its peril. If we fail to acknowledge the reality of crime, if we insist on viewing defendants as mere objects to be acted upon, we will be doomed to a vicious circle of crime and repression and more crime.

Most proposals for getting tough on crime mask the painful facts and difficult choices our country must face before we can meaningfully address the crime problem. We cannot frame the issues—let alone resolve them—until we develop and consider all the relevant facts and competing considerations. . . .

Too often a false dichotomy is created between those who care about the rights of criminal defendants and those who care about victims of crime. Reality is complicated, not black and white. Most offenders and most victims share a common background, come from the same neighborhoods; where the defendant is devalued and the facts of his experience ignored, so also is the victim likely to be treated. In order to devise effective solutions to the problem, we must understand and address the problems that lead both to the criminal court. This does not require that we be blind to danger or allow criminals to prey upon us. It does require that we not succumb to comforting slogans. . . .

I do not suggest, of course, that poverty or racism equals crime. As a matter of fact only a small percentage of those who endure these social evils violate the law. What is amazing is that so many deprived Americans accept their lot without striking out. It seems fair to say that violent crime among these people would be much more prevalent but for influences such as religion, welfare and perhaps alcohol. I am astonished by those who point to the docile deprived and say, "Their conditions do not force them to break the law; why should those conditions force others to?" Society should be as alarmed by the silent misery of those who accept their plight as it is by the violence of those who do not. . . .

Accepting the full implications of what we know about street crime might require us to provide every family with the means to create the kind of home all human beings need. It might lead us to afford the job opportunities that pose for some the only meaningful alternative to violence. It might demand for all children a constructive education, a decent place to live, and proper pre- and postnatal nutrition. . . . More fundamentally, it might compel the eradication of racism and prejudice. . . .

In sum, changing legal procedures or building more prisons simply will not work.

Judge Bazelon was talking about the "losers." What about the "winners"? The rich crust at the top of society? The prosperous ones who commit white-collar crimes? Their behavior cannot be explained by poverty. If poverty were ended and jobs were available to all, would the rate of crime drop? Certainly those social goals should be pursued on their own merit. But not with the expectation that all crime would be ended.

As Professor Sutherland wrote: "The causes of crime lie within the values of the social system. Two persons who are ambitious and thwarted will respond differently; one will steal, the other will get an extra job or perhaps do without. What such persons have learned from those with whom they associate (and more fundamentally from the culture of their society) will determine which of these paths they choose."

Undoubtedly the opportunity to steal and the possible consequences of being caught will affect the choice made. But opportunities are often at hand, and the chance of being caught is rarely very great. Why then will the vast majority of people in some societies not even consider violating the law—either for white-collar or street crimes—while in other societies an equally large percentage will commit crimes whenever the chance comes up?

Many believe that crime exists in our country because of the fundamental values of our social system. Where profit is the goal of human endeavor any means to gain it will be seized. The pressures for "making it," and the indifference to any harm done to others in the mad scramble for coming out on top, surely contribute to criminal behavior.

Some sociologists see American involvement in mass violence abroad as a factor in criminality. Our wars and intervention in Southeast Asia, in Latin America, and in other parts of the world inevitably bring about indiscriminate killing, and the constant exposure of all Americans through the media to graphic depictions of those acts can scarcely have beneficial effects.

This book has looked at our society, noting what critics say is wrong with it and what aspects contribute to crime in America. Perhaps we need to look at ourselves too. We need to examine what we do to each other. When we see someone go wrong, someone doing harm, we need to think about such behavior and make a judgment. Is this the way we want to live? Is that what we want to be? Are profit and power all there is in this world? Can we stand by and watch the slow erosion of our humanity? Have we forgotten that we are supposed to care about one another?

Glossary

arson The malicious burning of another person's or one's own dwelling, a factory, church, ship, or other property. A felony.

bail Money the accused leaves with the court as a pledge that he or she will appear for trial. It is given in order to obtain the prisoner's release from prison until the trial. If the accused does not appear, the court keeps the money.

burglary Breaking and entering the dwelling of another, with intent to commit a felony, whether the act is carried out or not. In many states the definition is modified to cover such offenses committed in shops, factories, warehouses, and so forth. There are various degrees of the crime.

capital crimes Those which can be punished by death.

crime Defined in many of the penal codes as an act or omission forbidden by law and punishable upon conviction by death, imprisonment, or fine, or removal from office or disqualification to hold or enjoy an office or trust. A crime can be a violation of a public right or a violation of the rights of a person.

criminal assault A violent attack with physical means—by blows or with weapons.

criminologist   One who conducts scientific study of crime as a social phenomenon, of criminal investigation, of criminals, and of penal treatment.

due process of law   A person accused of a crime is entitled to due process of law, which means a fair hearing or trial.

embezzlement   The fraudulent taking of property by a person to whom it has been entrusted, as of an employer's money by his or her clerk or of public funds by the officer in charge.

felony   As declared by most federal and state laws, an offense punishable by death or confinement for more than one year in a federal or state prison.

fraud   The intentional twisting of the truth to induce another person to part with some valuable possession. It can also be a false representation of a matter of fact that deceives or is meant to deceive another so that the deceived person acts upon it to his or her legal injury. Deceitful advertising is one example of fraud that injures the consumer.

grand jury   A panel of between twelve and twenty-three citizens who decide if the government has enough evidence to justify a trial.

homicide   The killing of one person by another. Felonious homicide is either manslaughter or murder. Homicide is justifiable when a person kills another in the performance of a legal duty, as in duly executing a death sentence; by unavoidable necessity; or to prevent the commission of an atrocious crime. Homicide is excusable when the killing is without criminal intent and is done by accident or in self-defense. Neither justifiable nor excusable homicide involves any legal guilt or punishment.

indictment   A formal accusation from a grand jury to prosecute someone for a crime.

larceny   The unlawful taking and carrying away of property with the intent to defraud the rightful owner of it. The difference between grand larceny and petty larceny has to do with the amount stolen.

loan shark   One who lends money at very high or extortionate rates of interest, usually to people in trouble who are desperate for cash.

manslaughter   The unlawful killing of a human being without malice, express or implicit. It is called "involuntary" when the killing results from the commission of an unlawful act that is not a felony, or the doing of a lawful act in an unlawful manner. It's called "voluntary" when the killing results from a sudden passion due to sufficient provocation.

murder The offense of unlawfully killing a human being with malice aforethought, express or implied. In many states the offense is divided into two degrees, murder in the first degree being the more severely punished and restricted to those cases where the killing was willfully deliberate, premeditated, or especially cruel, or where it was done in the course of some heinous felony, as arson, rape, and so forth.

parole A conditional and revocable release, provided by statute, of a prisoner with an indeterminate or unexpired sentence. The same word is used to denote the period of such freedom.

probation A method of treating a person convicted of an offense. The person is not imprisoned but released on a suspended sentence under supervision and upon special conditions. Usually the person must report at stated intervals to an officer.

prosecutor The attorney who conducts proceedings, especially in a criminal case, in a court on behalf of the government.

rape Sex with another person, male or female, without that person's consent, effected by force, pressure, intimidation, or deception.

robbery The theft of property from a person done with violence or the threat of violence.

whistle-blower One who reports to the authorities or to the media wrongdoing within his or her organization or agency or company.

A Note on Sources

IF YOU look up "Crime and Criminals" in the Subjects Catalog of your public library, you may be dismayed to find the entries for this topic running to forty large pages, with three columns per page. It is one more piece of evidence to show how powerfully crime dominates the public mind and how much attention the experts and the popularizers have given it.

I must add that besides the information to be found in these volumes, every daily newspaper you pick up enlarges your knowledge. The stories include accounts of crimes just committed, wrongdoers jailed, people indicted, trials held, sentences given, appeals made, imprisonment begun, and on and on, endlessly it would seem. Since I wanted my book to be abreast of what's happening now, I had to follow the press carefully. Sometimes I was able to track significant criminal cases from the first newsbreak to the slamming of the cell door behind the convict.

In writing any such book as this, where the sources are so abundant, you have to be highly selective. If I had chosen to read all or most of the books listed in the library catalog, it would have been years before I'd be ready to write my own book. I decided first to read some general studies of crime and justice and then to focus on those aspects that seemed most important. I knew from the start I couldn't go into everything. For one reason, this book was not meant to be a one-volume encyclopedia of crime. And for another, some parts of the story interest me more than others, or I believe they are more significant for my readers.

Here then are the titles of many of the books I used. For an overview of the problem: Ramsey Clark, *Crime in America,* Simon & Schuster, 1970; Elliott Currie, *Confronting Crime: An American Challenge,* Pantheon, 1985; and Edwin M. Schur, *Our Criminal Society,* Prentice-Hall, 1969.

For readers interested in the psychology of criminal behavior, or its moral aspects, there is Abigail L. Rosenthal, *A Good Look at Evil,* Temple University Press, 1988; and Jack Katz, *Seductions of Crime,* Basic Books, 1988.

Street crime and violent crime usually crowd the press. Documentary histories of violence in America offer rich background on it from colonial times down to recent years. One such collection is Richard Hofstadter and Michael Wallace, eds., *American Violence,* Vintage, 1970; and another is Richard M. Brown, ed., *American Violence,* Prentice-Hall, 1970. More recent studies include Dan Archey and Rosemary Gartner, *Violence and Crime in Cross-National Perspective,* Yale, 1988; and Cynthia K. Gillespie, *Justifiable Homicide,* Ohio State, 1989. Lillian B. Rubin provides an analysis of one of the most controversial examples of violence in *Quiet Rage: Bernie Goetz in a Time of Madness,* Farrar, Straus & Giroux, 1986.

The literature on organized crime is abundant, in both scholarly studies and personal histories of the players. Those include Nicholas Pillegi, *Wise Guy: Life in a Mafia Family,* G. K. Hall, 1987; and Joseph Pistone and Richard Woodley, *Donnie Brasco: My Undercover Life in the Mafia,* NAL, 1988. One of the best broad studies is Howard Abadinsky, *The Criminal Elite,* Greenwood, 1983. It is thoroughly documented and makes available a vast amount of highly specialized research by many authorities. Shana Alexander, *The Pizza Connection,* Weidenfeld and Nicolson, 1988, and Ralph Blumenthal, *Last Days of the Sicilians,* Times Books, 1988, offer dramatic coverage of one gang and its operations. Another book veers away from the Mafia to highlight another ethnic group's entry into organized crime. It is Gerald Posner's *Warlords of Crime: Chinese Secret Societies, The New Mafia,* McGraw-Hill, 1988.

As the reader will have noted, much attention is given in this book to white-collar crime—partly because, until quite recently, it was rather neglected in the courts and in the press and partly because my own opinion is that it does infinitely more harm to us as individuals and as a society than the far better known forms of street crime.

The seminal study is Edwin H. Sutherland, *White Collar Crime: The Uncut Version,* Yale, 1983. The papers given at a symposium on the subject are collected in Peter Wickman and Timothy Daily, eds., *White Collar and Economic Crime,* Lexington Books, 1982. Excellent analyses appear in the following: John M. Johnson and Jack D. Douglas, eds., *Crime at the Top: Deviance in Business and the Professions,* Lippincott, 1978; Morton Mintz and Jerry S. Cohen, *America, Inc.,* Dell, 1971; Russell Mokhiber, *Corporate Crime and Violence: Big Business Power and the Abuse of the Public Trust,* Sierra, 1988; Ralph Nader and Mark J. Green, eds., *Corporate Power in America,* Penguin, 1977.

Many authors have done detailed and often highly dramatic studies of the crimes of a specific corporation or industry. These include Paul Brodeur, *Outrageous Misconduct: The Asbestos Industry on Trial,* Pantheon, 1985; Michael H. Brown's report on the chemical pollution of the environment, *The Toxic Cloud,* Perennial-Harper, 1988; Stephen Fenichel, *Other People's Money: The Rise and Fall of the OPM Leasing Services,* Anchor Doubleday, 1985; Douglas Frantz, *Levine & Co.: Wall Street's Insider Trading Scandal,* Avon, 1988; Diana B. Henriques, *The Machinery of Greed: Public Authority Abuse and What to Do About It,* Lexington Books, 1986; Robert A. Hutchinson, *Off the Books: Citibank and the World's Biggest Money Game,* Morrow, 1986; Penny Lernoux, *In Banks We Trust,* Anchor Doubleday, 1987; Morton Mintz, *At Any Cost: Corporate Greed, Women, and the Dalkon Shield,* Pantheon, 1985; and Larry C. White, *Merchants of Death: The American Tobacco Industry,* Beechtree Books, 1988.

It's significant that one scholar has recently studied the defense put up by those accused of white-collar crime. In *Defending White Collar Crime: A Portrait of Attorneys at Work,* Yale, 1985, Kenneth Mann takes an inside look at how the elite of the legal profession work to control information about their clients, especially the flow of harmful information to government investigators. The book raises ethical and policy questions for the bar and for justice.

It is hard to discuss crime without going into the American system of justice. You need to know something about the law, about the system of courts, about lawyers, judges, juries, and prosecutors. I found very useful for grasping the development of the law, Lawrence M. Friedman's *A History of American Law,* Touchstone, 1985. A much briefer and simpler account is given in a series of short lectures by professors of the Harvard Law School. It is Harold J. Berman, ed., *Talks on American Law,* Random House, 1961. A very different critical approach is in David L. Bazelon, *Questioning Authority: Justice and Criminal Law,* Knopf, 1988. Three books that make sweeping attacks upon the present system of justice, claiming it is heavily biased against the interests of the poor and oppressed, are Robert Lefcourt, ed., *Law Against the People,* Vintage, 1971; Anne Strick, *Injustice for All,* Penguin, 1978; and Gerry Spence, *With Justice for None,* Times Books, 1989.

What government prosecutors do is the subject of James B. Steward, *The Prosecutors: Inside the Offices of the Government's Most Powerful Lawyers,* Touchstone, 1988. The leading lawyers in private practice are described and assessed in Joseph C. Goulden, *The Superlawyers,* Weybright & Talley, 1971.

A critique of the whole system with proposals for bettering it is in David C. Anderson, *Crimes of Justice: Improving the Police, the Courts, the Prisons,* Times Books, 1988. How juries operate is in Seymour Wishman, *Anatomy of a Jury,* Penguin, 1987.

What happens when the accused is convicted and faces sentencing? The report of a U.S. commission for the study of incarceration is found in Andrew von Hirsch, *Doing Justice: The Choice of Punishments,* Hill & Wang, 1976. To learn about the most extreme forms of punishment, there is Leon S. Sheleff, *Ultimate Penalties, Capital Punishment, Life Imprisonment, Physical Torture,* Ohio State, 1988. Writings from inside the prison walls are collected in Judith A. Scheffler, ed., *Wall Tappings: An Anthology of Writings by Women Prisoners,* Northeastern, 1988.

And finally, I must acknowledge considerable help from the files of the *New York Times.* Its news stories, feature articles, columns, and op-ed pieces on crime were a valuable resource. Of course, I referred to other newspapers and periodicals as well, but the *New York Times* proved indispensable.

Index